THE STORY OF THE EARTH

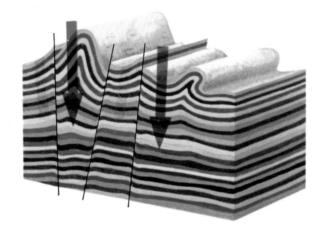

THE STORY OF THE EARTH

John Thackray

Ward Lock Limited · London

First published in Great Britain in 1980
by Ward Lock Limited, 116 Baker Street,
London W1M 2BB, a Pentos Company.

House editor Lesley Young
Text filmset in Monophoto Baskerville
by Asco Trade Typesetting Ltd., Hong Kong.

Printed and bound in Hong Kong by
South China Printing Co.

British Library Cataloguing in Publication Data

Thackray, John
 The story of the Earth.
 1. Earth—Juvenile literature
 I. Title
 550   QE29

ISBN 0-7063-5801-5

Contents

Part 1
PLANET
EARTH

The Earth in Space

As we travel around, we look out over city streets or country lanes, industrial complexes or river valleys. Our horizon may be 100 metres or 10 km distant, but we always feel at home in a world we know and understand.

Travelling in an aeroplane, land and sea are laid out for us just as on a map. We can trace the course of rivers from source to sea, and observe the patterns of industry and agriculture, highland and lowland. From a very high aeroplane or from a satellite orbiting the Earth, whole countries and even continents can be seen, and the curve of the Earth's surface becomes visible. Finally, from a space capsule the Earth is a beautiful blue and white ball suspended in jet-black space.

Our world seems very large to us, but compared with the vastness of space the Earth is very small indeed. Its radius is about 6,400 km (4,000 miles) and its circumference about 40,000 km (25,000 miles). It is not one-tenth of the size of any of the

Previous page Surtsey volcano in eruption off the coast of Iceland in 1963.

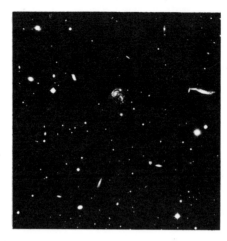

A cluster of galaxies in the constellation Hercules showing several different shapes, including spirals, barred spirals, and elliptical galaxies. These bodies are at least 1,000 million light-years away.

stars we see in the sky. On Earth a few thousand kilometres is a long journey. How small this seems compared to the 380,000 km (225,000 miles) that separate us from our closest neighbour in space, the Moon, or the 150 million km (93 million miles) we are from the Sun.

Astronomical distances are too large to measure in kilometres, so instead they are represented by the

time light takes to travel across them. Thus the Sun is said to be 8 light-minutes from the Earth because light takes 8 minutes to travel 150 million km (93 million miles). The Solar System, made up of the eight planets which, along with the Earth, orbit the Sun, is 11 light-hours in diameter. Distances to the stars are measured in light-years, one of these being almost 10 million million km (6 million million miles). Our closest star, Proxima Centauri, is 4 light-years away. Although on a clear night the sky looks packed with stars, they are really scattered very thinly, being several light-years apart. There are only eight stars within 10 light-years of us.

Stars are not sprinkled evenly through space but are arranged in great clusters, or galaxies. Our Galaxy has the shape of a disc, slightly thickened at the centre, made up of two spiralling arms. On a clear night the disc shows up as a band across the sky, in which stars seem crowded together; we call this the Milky Way. The Galaxy contains at least 100,000 million stars, as well as

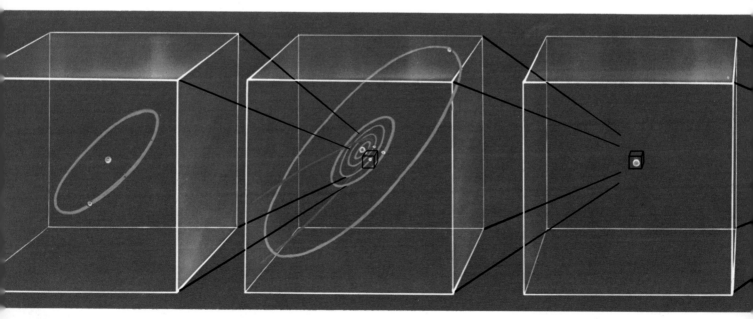

1

2

3

clouds of dust and gas, and is 100 light-years in diameter and 30 light-years thick at the centre. The Solar System is two-thirds of the way out from the centre, on the inner edge of one arm.

From this point distances become so great that our feeble imaginations will scarcely cope. Like stars, galaxies are also generally found in clusters. Our own is one of a cluster of thirty galaxies stretching for 5 million light-years. The nearest galaxy to us is Nubecula Major, 250,000 light-years away. Further out, 70 million light-years away, a cluster in the constellation Virgo contains a thousand or more galaxies. Fourteen galaxy clusters are known within 750 million light-years of Earth. The most distant known galaxies are 5,000 million light-years away from us.

Left A spiral galaxy made up of a thousand million stars in the constellation Canes Venatici. Our own galaxy has a similar shape though the arms probably spiral more tightly.

Below Six cubes, each having sides a thousand times longer than the one before, demonstrate the scale of the Earth in space. The cubes show: **1)** the Earth and Moon; **2)** the Solar System; **3)** the Sun in empty space; **4)** the nearest stars; **5)** the Galaxy; **6)** galaxies and galaxy clusters. The first is a one million km (600,000 miles) cube, and the last a 10 million light-year one.

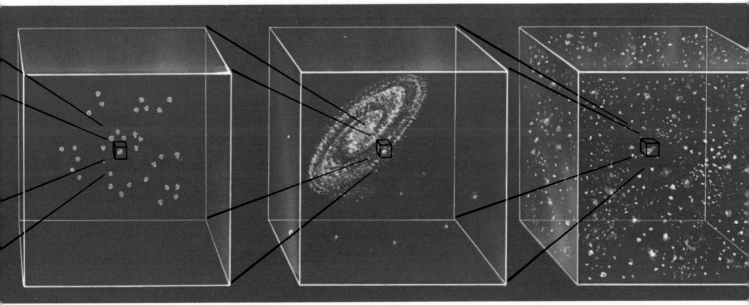

The Stars in the Sky

On a clear dark night hundreds of twinkling lights can be seen in the sky. These are some of the millions of stars that make up our Galaxy. They all have names, and many, such as the Plough, the Swan, Cassiopeia and the Pleiades are well-known constellations of the northern hemisphere. Each night the whole star pattern appears to rotate around a fixed point, marked by the Pole Star; in fact it is the stars which remain fixed while the Earth spins on its axis. Through the year a night-time observer sees a slightly different part of the sky each night as the Earth orbits the Sun. If the stars were visible during daylight, then during one year the Sun would be seen to pass once around the sky, cutting through twelve constellations in turn. These, the twelve Signs of the Zodiac, are named Aquarius, Capricorn, Sagittarius, Scorpio, Libra, Virgo, Leo, Cancer, Gemini, Taurus, Aries and Pisces.

In daylight the stars are hidden by blue light diffused in the sky, and only the Sun, itself a very ordinary star, is visible. Because we are only 150 million km (93 million miles) away, we can see its shape and surface features and benefit from its warmth and light. The other stars in the Galaxy are so distant that they are still only points of light when seen through the most powerful telescopes. Astronomers have found out about the stars principally by making precise measurements of their positions and apparent movements, and by analysing the light and other radiations that we receive from them.

As the Earth orbits the Sun the position of a nearby star will appear to change slightly relative to a more distant one. By measuring the angles involved and knowing the diameter of the Earth's orbit, the distance of the nearer star can be found by simple geometry known as the method of parallax. From the star's brightness and distance, its total energy output (luminosity) can be estimated. The light and invisible radiations gathered by a telescope from a particular star can be split up into their component parts by an instrument known as a spectroscope. By studying the spectrum that is produced, astronomers can work out the star's temperature, the elements on its surface, and the speed at which it is travelling relative to ourselves.

Some stars give out many times more energy than the Sun, others much less. Some are many times larger than the Sun, others smaller; some much hotter, others cooler. Some stars regularly change their luminosity (variable stars), others produce intermittent radiation (pulsars). From such observations comes our concept of the life history of a star, one type of which is outlined in the diagram below.

We often talk of the burning Sun, but nothing can actually burn in empty space. The energy of the stars comes from the fusion of atoms of hydrogen to form an atom of helium, and of helium to form more and more complex elements. The stars are really gigantic hydrogen bombs. The larger the star, the more complex the elements that can be formed within it. The heaviest elements found on Earth could not have formed within a star the size of the Sun, they must have come from an older and larger star which exploded, scattering its matter through space, just when our Sun and Solar System were beginning to form.

Is the formation of a system of orbiting planets a normal part of the life-history of a star, or is it a rare and accidental event? Nobody knows. We will probably never see another solar system, but there must be others somewhere in space.

It is believed the Solar System formed about 4,600 million years ago, and that our Galaxy is probably more than twice that age.

First step in the evolution of a massive star. Hydrogen gathers into a cloud and heats up as it contracts.

After 100 thousand years it will be a dense cloud shining brightly as its hydrogen turns into helium.

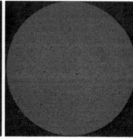

After 150 million years the hydrogen is used up and the star swells to become a red giant as heavy elements form.

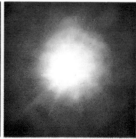

The star may explode, scattering matter through space.

The final stage is a small very dense star, emitting little light but strong radio waves.

a Kant-Laplace

1

2

3

4

b Jeans-Jeffreys

1

2

c Hoyle

1

3

4

2

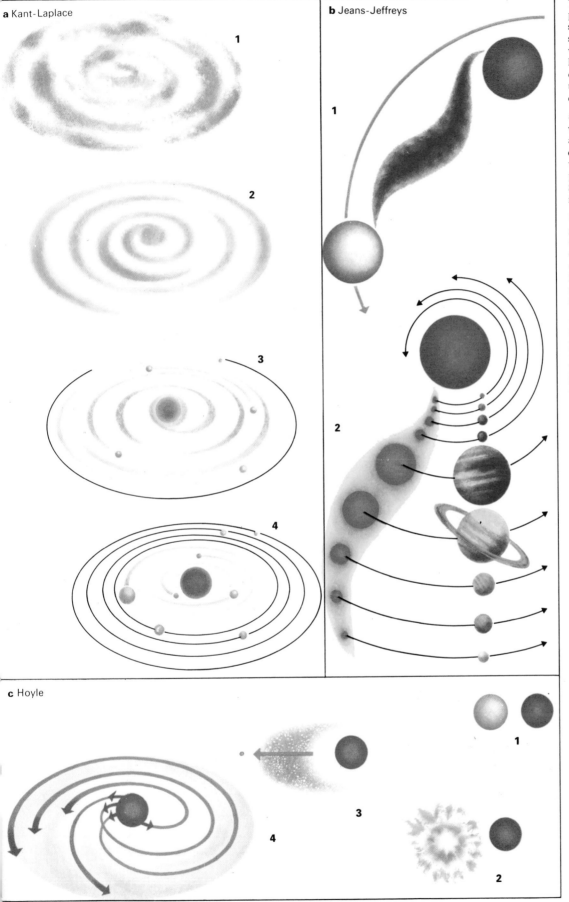

The fact that all the nine planets orbit the Sun in the same direction and in the same plane shows that the whole Solar System must have formed in a single event. There are three main theories, none of which is entirely satisfactory.

a) The 'nebular theory' is a very old one, suggesting that a vast revolving dust cloud contracted under its own weight to give the Sun and planets. On this theory the Sun should be spinning fast, which it is not.

b) Sir James Jeans suggested that a star passed close to the Sun, drawing out a filament of gas and dust which contracted to form the planets. This would mean that solar systems must be very rare in space.

c) Fred Hoyle suggested that the Sun was one of a pair of stars orbiting each other. The other star exploded, its debris contracting to form planets which then orbited the Sun.

11

The Moon and Planets

Among the stars are points of light, some very bright, some very dim, that are seen to move relative to the stars. These are the eight planets which orbit the Sun. The six inner planets, which include Earth, were known to the Ancient Greeks. William Herschel discovered Uranus in 1781; Neptune was first observed in 1846, and Pluto in 1930. Many astronomers suspect there is another large planet far beyond Pluto. If so it will only be visible through the largest telescopes. The planets look much like stars to the naked eye, but are really very different. They are all much closer and smaller than the stars, and they do not produce light of their own but merely reflect that emitted by the Sun. The planets move around the Sun along elliptical orbits at speeds depending on their distance from it. All but Pluto have their orbits more or less in the same plane, and all move around the Sun in the same direction.

Mercury is a small (diameter 4,840 km/3,000 miles), dense planet mostly composed of metals. It has a cratered surface with temperatures up to 350°C (590°F). It has no atmos-

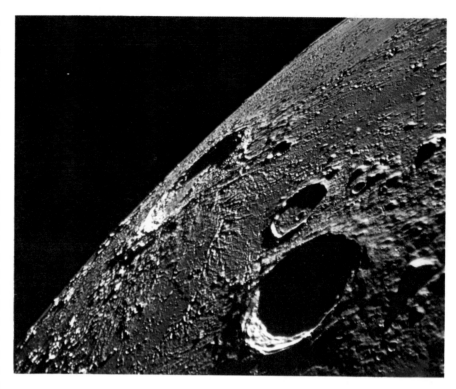

Above The surface of the Moon seen from the Apollo 12 Command Module. Moon craters formed when meteorites crashed into the surface during the early days of the Solar System, or were made by volcanoes, now long extinct. There is no erosion on the Moon, so its surface has remained undisturbed for millions of years. There is no life on the Moon.

Below A diagram showing the relative sizes and different appearances of the Sun and the planets. Drawn to this scale and in their correct positions, Earth would be 5·8 km (3·6 miles), and Pluto about 230 km (150 miles) from the Sun. Other members of the Solar System not shown here are the satellites, asteroids and comets.

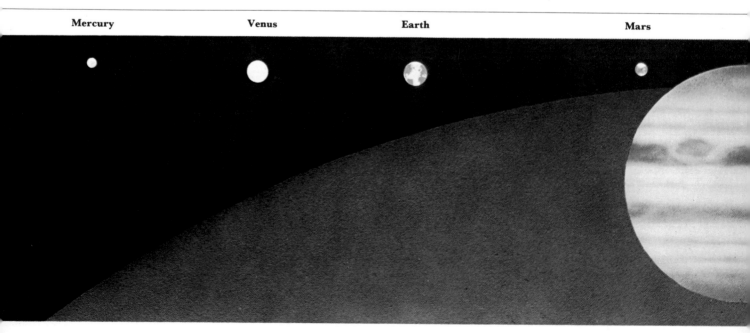

Mercury   Venus   Earth   Mars

phere. It orbits the Sun once every 70 Earth days, and spins so slowly that its day lasts 176 Earth days.

Venus is a small (diameter 12,200 km/7,700 miles), dense planet, similar in structure to Earth. Its thick and cloudy atmosphere of carbon dioxide obscures the surface whose temperature rises to 400°C (750°F). It orbits the Sun once every 225 Earth days.

Earth is the largest inner planet (diameter 12,756 km/7,927 miles), and has a metallic core surrounded by layers of silicate rock. Much of the surface is covered with water, and there is an atmosphere of nitrogen and oxygen which supports life. It orbits the Sun once every 365¼ Earth days; surface temperatures vary between +60°C (+140°F) and −90°C (−130°F). It has a satellite, the Moon, which orbits Earth once every 27·3 Earth days. The Moon is 3,476 km (2,158 miles) in diameter, and has only one-sixth of the Earth's field of gravity. There is no atmosphere, water, or life, and its cratered surface has changed little in 2,500 million years.

Mars is a small (diameter 6,760 km/ 4,190 miles), dense planet, with a polar ice-cap and an atmosphere of carbon dioxide. The surface shows signs of meteorite impacts, volcanic eruptions, erosion and deposition.

There is no evidence of life. Mars has two small satellites.

Jupiter is the biggest planet (diameter 142,700 km/88,700 miles) and is probably largely made up of hydrogen and helium, perhaps with a central rocky or metallic core. It is three times as far from the Sun as Mars and has fourteen satellites.

Saturn is a large (diameter 120,800 km/75,000 miles) low-density planet made up of light gases around a rocky core. The rings which revolve around the globe are made of small fragments of ammonia ice. Saturn has ten satellites.

Uranus is a large (diameter 46,700 km/29,300 miles) low-density planet. It has a greenish tinge, probably due to methane in its atmosphere. It is 2,800 million km (1,700 million miles) from the Sun and has a surface temperature of −190°C (−310°F). It has two satellites.

Neptune is a large (diameter 49,900 km/31,200 miles) planet, similar in character to Uranus, but denser. It orbits the Sun each 165 Earth years.

Pluto is the most distant planet so far discovered. Its existence was predicted from certain irregularities in the orbit of Neptune. Pluto's orbit is strongly eccentric and is inclined to the orbits of the other planets. It is thought to be smaller and denser than Earth.

A rocket being launched as part of a programme of space exploration.

Jupiter   Saturn   Uranus   Neptune   Pluto

Meteors and Meteorites

Between the orbits of Mars and Jupiter lie the asteroids. These rocky and metallic fragments, some 40,000 in number, range in size from the minor planet Ceres, diameter 680 km (427 miles), to irregular lumps a metre or less across. Most have roughly circular orbits around the Sun, but a few move very eccentrically and come close enough to be captured by Earth's field of gravity.

Such a fragment enters Earth's atmosphere at up to 70 km (45 miles) per second. Friction with the air heats the fragment, melting, vaporizing or breaking it up. The bright light caused by this is called a meteor or shooting star, and the explosion may be seen as a brilliant fireball. If the fragment is large it will not be entirely destroyed and pieces called meteorites will land on Earth. Passage through the air melts the outer layers of a meteorite, which often has a black, glassy crust and rounded flow-shapes on the surface. Often a meteorite breaks into angular fragments before landing, so the black crust is generally incomplete. A fragment of over 100 tonnes would be travelling so fast when it landed that the energy released would turn most of it to vapour.

Although several thousand fragments enter Earth's atmosphere daily, few survive, and only about ten are collected each year. The light and sound effects of a fall are impressive. The brilliant white meteor is first seen, followed by a thin white dust cloud as the light disappears. Then comes noise like thunder and a loud roaring. Meteorites are found on or just below ground surface, and are always hot to the touch. It is untrue that they are especially prone to fall during thunderstorms, though because of their particular orbits and the rotation of the Earth, most do fall in the afternoon and early evening.

Above Hoba West Meteorite. An iron meteorite weighing 60 tonnes, the heaviest known.

Left Meteor Crater, Arizona was formed 20,000 years ago by a gigantic meteorite which vaporized on impact.

Opposite, above An exploding meteorite. A member of the Andromedid shower, photographed in 1895.

Meteorites are of three main types: stones, irons and stony-irons. Stony meteorites are made of a crystalline igneous rock that looks a bit like a pale, fine-grained granite. They are made up of familiar minerals, such as olivine, felspar, enstatite and hypersthene, but many also contain tiny mineral blobs called chondrules, unlike anything in terrestrial rocks. All stony meteorites are very similar in composition and have a characteristic pale greenish tinge, often with rusty-brown streaks. The rock is soft and weathers away to dust if exposed for long. One interesting type contains traces of organic materials such as hydrocarbons and amino acids. When first discovered it was suggested there must have

been life among the asteroids. It is now thought 'contamination' occurred after landing.

Iron meteorites are alloys in which iron is mixed with up to 20 per cent nickel. The metals lie in very complex intergrown crystals, shown as feathery patterns, known as Widmanstätten structures, when a polished surface is etched.

Stony-iron meteorites are an intermediate group in which grains of silicate minerals lie in a groundmass of nickel-iron alloy.

Most meteorites seen to fall and collected soon afterwards are stones, fewer than one in ten being irons or stony-irons. Museum collections, however, usually contain many more irons than stones, because a lump of nickel-iron alloy is more resistant to weathering and more obvious than a soft grey igneous rock that looks like granite.

Among many objects often confused with meteorites are ironstone concretions, iron pyrite nodules, and artificial slags.

The largest known meteorite lies in the ground at Hoba West in Namibia. It is an iron meteorite unusually rich in nickel, and weighs 60 tonnes. Surprisingly there is no sign of any crater; perhaps the meteorite fell so long ago that all trace of it has been eroded. The most impressive meteorite crater on Earth is near Winslow, Arizona, USA. More than 1 km (nearly 1 mile) wide and 130 m (400 ft) deep, it was probably formed 20,000 years ago. The original meteorite, which must have weighed several hundred tonnes was largely vaporized by the force of the impact, and no large pieces have been found in the bowl. This crater is small compared with most on the Moon, many of which were formed 3,000 million years ago by meteorites weighing thousands of tonnes. The Moon has no atmosphere so there would be no meteor effects and speeds of impact would be much higher than on Earth. Langrenus is a typical large crater, 135 km (85 miles) in diameter, and 3 km (9,000 ft) deep.

The only large and destructive

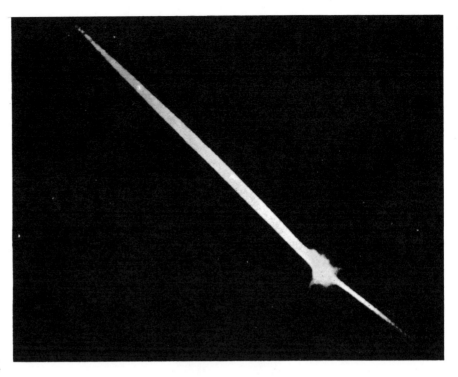

The Asteroid belt, between Mars and Jupiter, contains at least 40,000 rocky and metallic fragments, a few of which are captured by the Earth's gravity each year.

fall recorded on Earth happened in Siberia in 1908. Bright flashes and loud noises were widely recorded and pine trees were blown down over hundreds of square kilometres. An expedition to the site soon after found no trace of a meteorite, only a series of small craters. Whether the damage was caused by a large meteorite which vaporized, or the head of a small comet is uncertain.

While it is generally accepted that meteorites originated in the asteroid belt, there are two theories for the origin of the asteroids. The first is that there was originally a large planet between Mars and Jupiter having, like Earth, a metallic core and a rocky mantle. This planet broke up a long while ago, leaving thousands of fragments in orbit around the Sun. Iron meteorites are pieces of the core, stones are from the mantle, and stony-irons are from the junction of the two. The second theory is that the asteroids are remains of the original debris clouds from which the Solar System formed, and that there never was a planet in the orbit they now occupy. Whichever theory is correct, meteorites certainly date from the time of formation of the Solar System. All seem to be about 4,600 million years old, also the age of the oldest Moon rocks and the suspected age of Earth.

Jupiter
asteroids
Mars
Earth
Venus
Mercury
Sun

Introduction to the Earth

The Earth is the largest of the four inner members of the Solar System. It orbits the Sun at a distance of about 150 million km (93 million miles), in the middle of the zone around the Sun where the temperature is neither too hot nor too cold for life to exist. Mars is on the outer edge of this zone and Venus on the inner. The Earth is large and dense enough to be able to hold an envelope of gas, the atmosphere, around itself, which has led to the build up of surface water, and the development of life. In this Earth is unique in the Solar System.

Earth is a sphere of rock, metal and water, 12,756 km (7,927 miles)

Left The four seasons. Diagrams showing the tilt of the Earth's axis of rotation relative to the Sun's rays at the June solstice, the September equinox, the December solstice and the March equinox. Notice the sunlight received by the Earth's Poles at the two solstices, and the positions of the Tropics of Cancer and Capricorn at the equinoxes.

Below The Earth from space. A photograph showing Africa and the Near East taken on the Apollo 11 space mission.

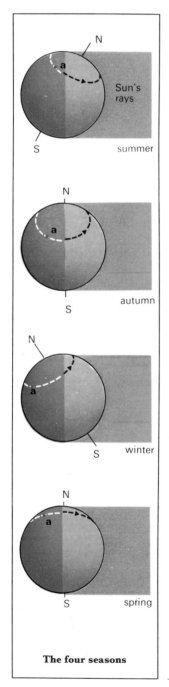

The four seasons

in diameter and 40,075 km (24,920 miles) in circumference at the Equator. It orbits the Sun at a speed of 100,000 km (66,000 miles) per hour, completing one circuit every $365\frac{1}{4}$ days. At the same time it spins around its own axis, taking 23 hours 56 minutes for one complete turn. These movements are not apparent to us. The spin of the Earth causes the alternating light and dark of day and night. During the day the Sun appears to move across the sky from east to west, while at night the stars seem to circle a point to the north, marked by the Pole Star in the northern hemisphere, and to the south in the southern hemisphere. These movements are illusions.

The axis of the Earth's spin is not vertical to its orbit around the Sun but is tilted at an angle of $23\frac{1}{2}°$. This tilt causes the seasons. For half the year the northern hemisphere is tilted towards the Sun. Here day will be longer than night and the Sun will be higher in the sky than in winter; around the North Pole it will never set. The tilt towards the Sun increases until the Summer solstice is reached on 21 June, when the $23\frac{1}{2}°$ tilt is directed straight at the Sun. This is midsummer in the northern hemisphere, midwinter in the southern. The midday Sun is then vertically overhead on a line around the Earth called the Tropic of Cancer, 2,500 km (1,500 miles) north of the Equator. As the Earth continues its orbit the tilt decreases until the equinox is reached in September, when the axis of rotation is vertical relative to the Sun and the midday Sun is overhead around the Equator. From then on the southern hemisphere tilts towards the Sun, bringing winter in the north and perpetual darkness around the North Pole.

The eccentricity of the Earth's orbit has a small effect on the seasons. The Earth is 148 million km ($91\frac{1}{2}$ million miles) from the Sun in December and nearly 151 million km ($93\frac{1}{2}$ million miles) in July. This tends to give the southern hemisphere shorter, hotter summers and

The force of gravity pulls this parachutist down to Earth. The air resistance on his parachute slows down his fall and will save his life.

longer, colder winters than the north. This effect is largely masked by the differences in distribution of land and sea in the two hemispheres.

The way we estimate time is based on the movements of the Earth. Seconds, minutes and hours are subdivisions of a day, which is very close to the time taken for one revolution of the Earth on its axis. The calendar year of 365 days is rather shorter than the time taken for one orbit of the Sun, so every four years we have a leap year of 366 days. The month is based loosely on the $29\frac{1}{2}$ days from one full moon to the next.

The force which keeps the planets in their orbits and our feet on the ground is gravity which acts between two or more bodies, tending to draw them together. The larger and closer the bodies, the greater the force. We weigh what we do on Earth because our own mass and the 6,600 million million million tonnes of the Earth exert a gravitational pull on each other. At 1,000

km up in space above Earth we would weigh less because the distance between the two bodies is increased. Standing on the Moon we would weigh only one-sixth of our Earth-weight because the Moon is correspondingly smaller than the Earth.

A second invisible force field makes Earth a giant magnet. Earth's magnetic poles are close to the geographic poles and are not fixed but move slowly around. The magnetic field is caused by movements in the metallic core at the centre of the Earth. It is because of this field that compass needles align themselves north–south, but, more important, dangerous radiations and rays are deflected and trapped high above the Earth in regions called the Van Allen belts. Without this life would be impossible.

Inside the Earth

Earth is made up of a number of layers of different materials, one inside the other. In the centre is an inner core of solid metal, and this is surrounded successively by the outer core of liquid metal; the very thick mantle, made of rock; the thin crust, itself in two parts; a thin layer of water in some places, and an atmosphere of gas.

Since the deepest oil wells do not penetrate more than about 8 km

(5 miles) or so, our knowledge of these layers is incomplete. Studies of the way earthquake waves travel through the Earth have given us most of our information. The various types of waves travel at different speeds through different rocks, and change direction as they pass from one layer to another. Certain waves—shake waves—travel without difficulty through solid rock, but will not pass through li-

quid. Recording stations all over the world pick up waves triggered off by an earthquake and by noting the times of arrival of different types of waves in different areas, their speed of travel in different parts of the Earth's interior can be worked out. From this information we can also estimate the type of rock present.

The core of the Earth is thought to be made of nickel-iron alloy, rather similar to iron meteorites in composition. The outer part is known to be liquid from the fact that earthquake S-waves will not pass through the Earth to a depth greater than 3,000 km (1,900 miles). The inner core is even hotter than the outer, up to 10,000°C (18,000°F) at the centre, but is probably solid metal because of the tremendous pressure it is under.

The mantle is thought to consist mainly of a dense, dark-coloured rock called peridotite, which is made up of the two silicate minerals olivine and pyroxene. Peridotite has properties which agree with those suggested by the behaviour of the earthquake waves; it is also found at four places on the Earth, Cyprus being one, where the mantle has broken through the crust to appear at the surface. The temperature of the mantle varies from 1,500°C (2,700°F) at the top to 6,000°C (10,800°F) where it meets the core. The rock of Earth's mantle is not liquid, but neither is it hard and brittle like rock at the surface of the Earth. It is very hot and under great pressure, and will bend and flow if sufficient force is applied for a sufficiently long time. In some zones it will become

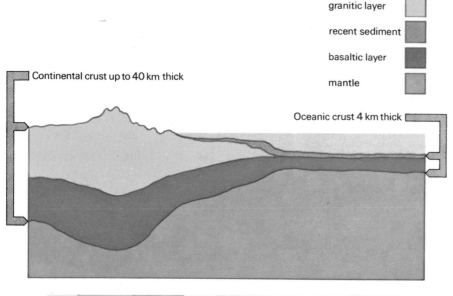

granitic layer
recent sediment
basaltic layer
mantle

Continental crust up to 40 km thick

Oceanic crust 4 km thick

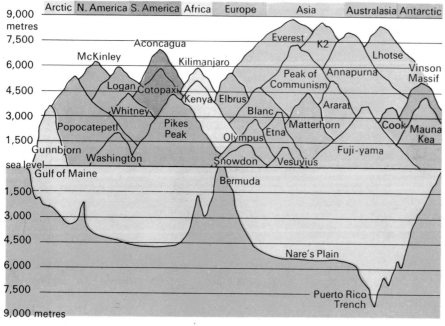

Above left A section through the outermost layers of the Earth, showing the upper mantle, basaltic and granitic crusts and water.

Left A relief map of the Earth's surface showing the highest mountains compared with the ocean deeps.

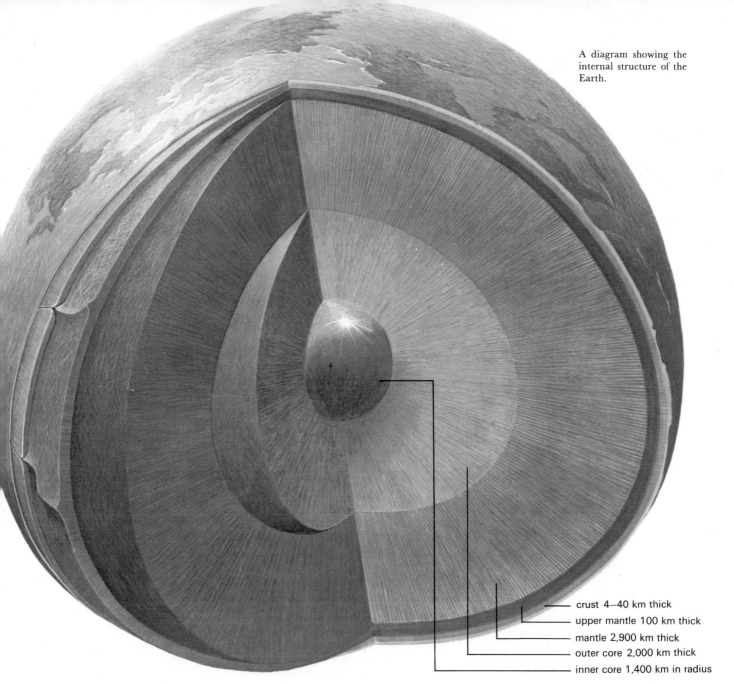

crust 4–40 km thick
upper mantle 100 km thick
mantle 2,900 km thick
outer core 2,000 km thick
inner core 1,400 km in radius

liquid for limited periods, providing raw material for volcanic lava.

The crust is the layer of rock on which we live, and which geologists study. It is thinner in relation to the Earth than the skin is to an apple. The junction of crust and mantle is known as the Moho and is one of the places where earthquake waves change direction. The crust is of two sorts, basaltic and granitic, sometimes called 'sima' and 'sial' respectively. Basaltic crust is a continuous layer around the Earth about 6 km (4 miles) thick, made of the dark, fairly dense rocks basalt and dolerite. Where it is covered by granitic crust it is generally thicker and the rocks are altered by heat and pressure into amphibolite. The granitic crust is not a continuous layer but a number of separate slabs of light-coloured less-dense rocks such as granite and gneiss. Each slab has a very complicated history and structure and includes sedimentary, volcanic, igneous and metamorphic rocks of many different types. Slabs of granitic crust, riding like rafts on the basaltic crust, are known as continents; lower-lying areas of basaltic crust are called ocean basins.

By a coincidence, the amount of water on the Earth's surface almost exactly fills the ocean basins, just a small bit spilling on to the edges of the continents to form the shelf seas.

It used to be thought that Earth's internal heat was left over from the time when the Earth was formed and was entirely molten. It is now thought that although the Earth may have been molten for a short time, the main source of heat is the many radioactive elements present in the rocks of the crust and mantle. As the elements decay they produce heat which maintains the high temperature of the core and mantle. The most important elements are uranium and potassium.

The Dynamic Earth

The Earth is not a quiet unchanging object, but is restless and alive with movement right to its centre.

We have seen that movements of molten metal in the Earth's core are responsible for the magnetic field that protects us from radiation. The core is so hot that it causes movements of rock in the mantle by convection. Convection can be seen in a pan of water warming on a stove: hot water at the bottom is less dense than cold water at the surface, so the hot rises and the cold sinks. The hot water cools at the surface while the cold warms up at the bottom, and a continuous circulation is set up. At its base the mantle has a temperature of 6,000°C (10,800°F), while at the top it is only 1,500°C (2,700°F). The difference in density between rocks at these two temperatures is sufficient to force the stiff but pliable rock into motion. Because movements are very slow, regular convection cells are set up, unlike the jumbled movements in the water pan. There are eight of these cells in existence at the moment, each one consisting of an elongated rising current which rolls over at the top of the mantle and moves horizontally for a while before dropping down to complete its circuit.

Many of the effects of these currents are visible on the surface of the Earth. Lines along which hot currents are rising are the underwater mountain ranges known as mid-ocean ridges, while the lines where the cooling current drops downwards are often marked by deep clefts in the ocean floor known as ocean trenches. Ridges and trenches are where most of the world's earthquakes and volcanic eruptions occur; these are the active zones of the Earth. They are the boundaries of enormous areas that are relatively stable, known as plates. The whole concept of convection currents, or mantle motion, and their effects is known as the theory of plate tectonics.

As it reaches the top of the mantle, the rising current of rock divides and flows out to each side. Basaltic crust is welded on to the mantle and so the ocean floor spreads outwards on each side of the mid-ocean ridge. This is known as sea-floor spreading. Along the ridge molten rock rises to form new basaltic crust as these movements occur and the ocean floor is constantly being formed along the ridges. As it sinks down into the mantle at the line of the ocean trench, the current of rock takes the basaltic crust with it into the depths. The ocean floor is constantly being destroyed along the trenches.

Meanwhile the low-density continents remain floating like rafts of granite. They move hither and thither with the basaltic crust on which they sit. They may crumple as they collide or as they push against a down-current of mantle, and may split if an up-current rises from beneath, but they are not easily created or destroyed. All these movements are very slow—about 2–10 cm (1–5 in) yearly. Only after a million or so years do real changes in Earth's geography become apparent.

Below Map of ridges, plates and trenches, with indications of some directions of movement.

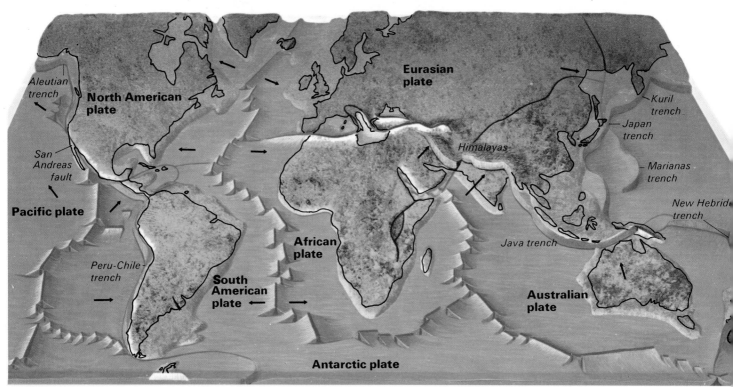

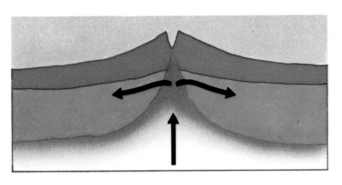

1 A mid-ocean ridge

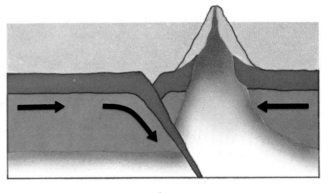

2 A deep-ocean trench with volcano

Convection currents
in the Earth

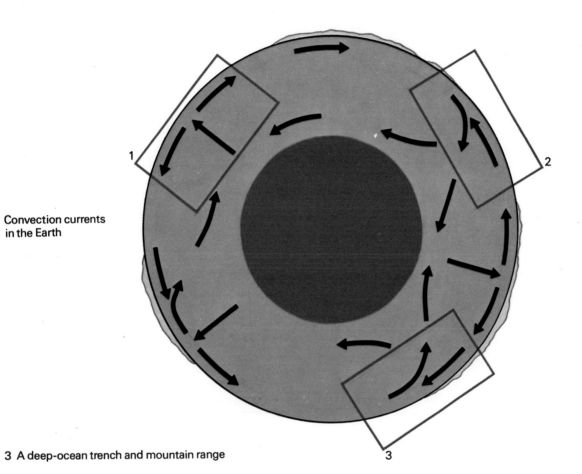

3 A deep-ocean trench and mountain range

Granitic crust

Basaltic crust

Mantle

Hot rock

Core

Convection currents in the Earth's mantle and some of their effects on the surface.

Exploring the Oceans

Nearly three-quarters of the surface of the Earth is covered by water, and almost all of it is in the great open water system of the oceans. The whole mass of water is interconnected, though the Pacific, Indian, Atlantic, Arctic and Antarctic oceans are separately named.

The amount of water in the ocean system—1,300 million cubic km (510 million cubic miles)—fills the low-lying areas between the granitic continents that geologists call the ocean basins, overflowing on to the extreme edge of the continents in what are known as shelf seas. Hudson Bay and the English Channel are both shelf seas—indeed Britain is surrounded by shelf sea.

A typical ocean has a shelf sea at its edge which may be 10 or 100 km wide, but which is no more than 180 metres (500 ft) deep. Its floor is made up of granitic and sedimentary rocks just like those of the land. Then comes the continental slope which marks the edge of the granitic crust and which runs at a steepness of about one in ten until the ocean floor is reached at about 3,500

Right A diver, equipped to explore the shallow shelf seas. Specially strengthened submarines can be used in deep water.

Below The age of rocks on the floor of the Atlantic Ocean, showing how they spread out from the ridge.

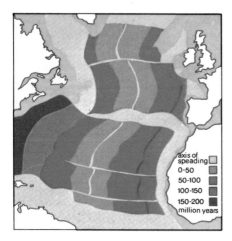

axis of
spreading
0-50
50-100
100-150
150-200
million years

metres (10,000 ft). The deep trenches go down to 11,000 metres (7 miles), while the ocean ridges stand up to 1,200 metres (4,000 ft) high.

The most noticeable features of the oceans to seaside visitors are waves and tides. Waves are formed

in the open by the action of the wind. In open water a wave moving along just bobs the water up and down; only when the wave breaks on the shore does water rush forward in a foaming mass. Tides, on the other hand, are caused by the

gravitational pull of the Moon. The Moon orbits the Earth every 24 hours 50 minutes, and twice within that period there will be a high tide at any one place. Depending on local conditions the tidal rise may be 5 metres (15 ft) or as much as 12 metres (36 ft). Especially high tides come when the weaker gravitational pull of the Sun backs up that of the Moon; this happens at the times of new and full Moon. A third feature of the ocean waters, not visible at the seaside, is the great ocean currents. These are broadly circular movements of water within the main ocean caused by the prevailing winds. The Gulf Stream, for example, moves around the north and western edges of the North Atlantic Ocean, and the Canaries Current completes the circle to the south.

The floor of the ocean is usually covered with anything up to 2 km (1 mile) of very fine sediment made up of the skeletons of minute animals and plants that live in the surface waters and of very fine mud particles carried down off the continents by water currents. A sediment found at the edge of the oceans is the muddy sand, known as turbidite, which forms when underwater avalanches pour down the long continental slopes at high speed, spreading a layer of turbid water for several kilometres.

Below these sediments are the layers of basalt and dolerite that form the top of the crust. Along the ocean ridges these rocks make up the ocean floor, sediment being present only in pockets. When these rocks are dated it is found that the ones on the oceanic ridges are very young, and that they get steadily older away towards the trenches. Even the oldest of these rocks are no more than 250 million years old. This confirms our idea that the sea-floor is spreading out from the ridges. The mid-ocean ridges are areas of earthquake and volcanic activity; Iceland, the Azores and Tristan da Cunha are well-known volcanic islands on the mid-Atlan-

tic ridge. The deep trenches are also prone to earthquake and volcano; the arc-shaped lines of volcanoes which run from the Aleutian Islands in the north Pacific down to New Zealand in the south are all on the inner edges of trenches.

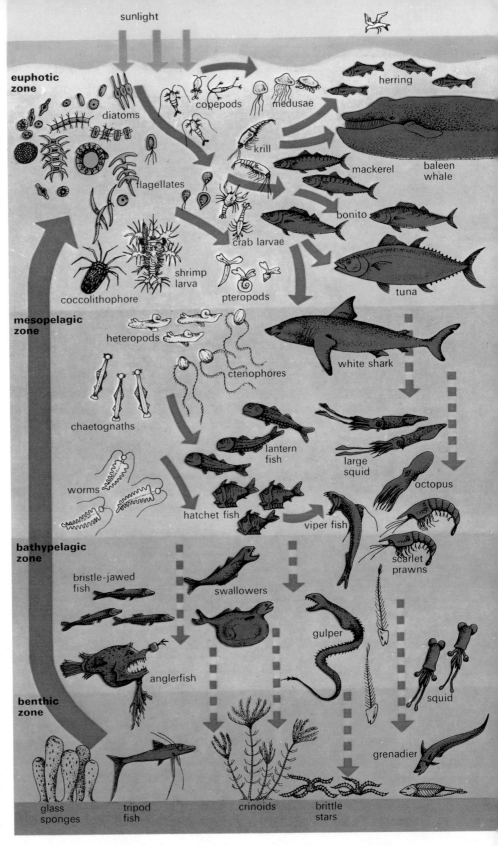

The ecology of the oceans. Floating plants (*top left*), are eaten by floating animals (*top centre*), which are eaten by swimming animals (*top right and centre*). Dead organisms of all sorts fall to the seabed, where they decay into simple chemicals which are carried to the surface by up-welling water currents.

23

The Continents

Just over one-quarter of the Earth's surface is made up of land, nearly all of it being within the six great continents of North America, South America, Africa, Europe and Asia (sometimes called Eurasia), Australia and Antarctica. These are the six great slabs of granitic crust that were mentioned on page 19. The only lands which are not in some way part of these continents are the volcanic islands which rise up from the ocean floor. In contrast to the oceans which are still largely unknown, there are few land areas that are inaccessible or unexplored.

The land surface is endlessly variable. In each area particular animals and plants have become adapted to the conditions of climate and relief, so that no two parts of the world are exactly the same. At the South Pole is the frozen wasteland of the Antarctic, while elsewhere are found mountain ranges, rolling grassy or forested hills, endless flat grassy plains, arid deserts and tropical jungles. Most of the food we eat and most of the minerals and other raw materials we use come from the land.

Geologically speaking, there are some important differences between the continents and the oceans. We have seen on page 18 the difference in the thickness and composition of the crust in these two areas, and we learnt on page 23 that the ocean floor is made up of very young rocks. The oldest rocks so far discovered on land are about 3,800 million years old, nearly as old as the Earth itself. They come from West Greenland and include a pebbly rock called conglomerate which shows that even at this early date there was running water on the land. These oldest rocks are only found in a few places, but many areas have rocks that are about 3,000 million years old. These ancient rocks show that, while the ocean floor is constantly being produced and renewed, the continents are permanent features of the Earth. It seems that the continents were once smaller than they are now and have been growing throughout Earth's long and eventful history.

The ocean-floor rocks show a very simple age-pattern on both sides of the ocean ridge. Rocks on

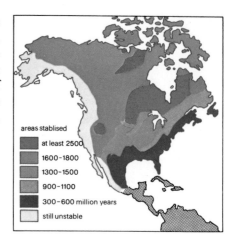

areas stablised

at least 2500
1600–1800
1300–1500
900–1100
300–600 million years
still unstable

Above A map showing the structure of the continent of North America with its core of ancient rock surrounded by successively younger tracts. The youngest of the five tracts is an active mountain range, the Rocky Mountains.

land also show an age-pattern, though it is not quite so easy to spot. The most ancient rocks are generally grouped in the centre of the continent, while younger rocks are arranged around them, something like the rings of a tree. The outermost and youngest ring is often a mountain range which is still being formed. The rings of medium age were formed as mountain ranges

hundreds of millions of years ago and are now being worn down to ranges of rolling hills. The very ancient core, known as a shield, is usually low-lying and may be covered by thin layers of more recent flat-lying rock.

Another contrast between the geology of the continents and oceans is in the variety of rock types to be found. The ocean floor is largely made of very fine-grained sediments and basaltic lavas; the continents display a baffling array of rocks of many different compositions and origins. This is partly due to the greater age of the continents and partly to the constant cycle of erosion, deposition and uplift described on page 20. The granite which must have made up the primeval continents has been completely altered by these processes.

Long before the discovery of seafloor spreading and convection currents in the mantle, it was thought by some geologists that the continents were not fixed in their positions but were drifting. Evidence from the shapes of the continents, from the distribution of certain types of fossils, and from the pattern of ancient climates, suggested that 250 million years ago the continents were joined in a single enormous landmass. These ideas have been confirmed by the discovery of seafloor spreading, and the theory of continental drift is now well established. The movements of the continents, with their collisions and tearings apart, have been followed, in broad outline, through the last 600 million years, and can even be predicted for the future. In 50 million years, Africa will probably have pushed northwards, closing the Mediterranean Sea, Australia and New Zealand will be on the Equator and California will be an island!

Left Flat farmland in Colorado, USA.

Right Mountainous terrain with traces of ancient man in Peru. These mountains, the Andes, are the youngest of a number of great rocky tracts that make up South America.

Mountain Ranges

Asia can boast Earth's highest mountain, Mount Everest in the Himalayas, which is 8,850 m (29,000 ft) high, but all the other continents except Antarctica have peaks which exceed 4,000 m (12,000 ft). Mountains are often capped with permanent fields of snow and ice because the air is rarified at high altitudes and so is less able to transform the sun's rays into warmth. As the air is thin and clear these rays still tan the skin, and indeed climbers can suffer sunburn and frostbite together.

On the slopes of any mountain it gets colder as you climb upwards, and a series of climatic bands can be recognized. A typical mountain might have five bands, the lowest being a deciduous forest of oak and ash, the next a forest of fir trees, and the next a grassy band with small flowering plants and stunted bushes. Above this comes a barren rocky band with tufts of grass, moss and lichen and occasional mountain sheep and goats. Above again is the band of perpetual snow and ice. The height of these different bands depends on the latitude of the mountain range. The line of perpetual snow is at 3,000 m (9,000 ft) in the Alps, but at 6,000 m (18,000 ft) in tropical Africa. Partly because of this change in climate and partly because soil is easily washed away by heavy rain, mountains are often rocky places.

A number of famous mountains are volcanoes, made of sloping layers of lava and volcanic ash which have erupted from underground. Vesuvius, Etna and Fujiyama are three examples. Volcanoes are usually conical, and are geologically rather young, being rarely more than one million years old, though remains of very ancient ones, now worn flat, are known.

A second type of mountain is the block mountain, a small range which stands abruptly above the surrounding plain from which it is separated by a great crack or fault. These seem to have been pushed up from below by some means not yet understood. The Sierra Nevada in North America and the Ruwenzori Mountains in East Africa are examples. They are generally made of layers of sedimentary rock, flat-lying or only gently folded, and are usually found within a continent rather than at its edge.

All Earth's major mountain ranges—the Rockies, Andes, Alps, Urals and Himalayas—are fold mountains. The ranges are usually long and narrow; the Andes are 6,000 km (4,000 miles) long and never more than 500 km (300 miles) wide. The rocks are folded and faulted into very complex structures so that even their original order may be hard to discern. The rock are also often altered by heat and pressure so that their original sedimentary characters are lost. The major folds usually run down the length of the mountain ranges and the most severely altered rocks are in the centre. Sedimentary rocks in fold mountains tend to be much thicker than those of similar age on neighbouring plains, and were often laid down in deep water. High ranges often suffer severe earthquakes and volcanic eruptions.

At one time it was thought that as the Earth cooled it shrank and wrinkled like an old apple, causing these ranges, but we now know that it has not cooled much over the short period in which the world's highest mountains have formed. The cause lies once again in the plate structure of the Earth. Where a slab of continental crust is pushed against a cold current of ocean crust which is dropping down into the mantle, the continental crust is very slowly crumpled, broken and even melted in places, and finally pushed up to form a high mountainous range (see page 20). This is how the Rockies and the Andes formed, and indeed are still forming, for earthquakes and volcanic eruptions still raise up the land.

Mountain ranges within a continent formed as two slabs of granitic crust collided. A wide ocean once separated Europe from Asia down the line of the Urals; 250 million years ago the two continents collided at a combined speed of 3 or 4 cm (2 in) per year. This immense force was sufficient to raise a mountain chain that is still 1,600 m (4,500 ft) high. India was an island until about 20 million years ago when it collided with the southern edge of Asia and, pushing below it, raised the Himalayas.

The lines of many ancient mountain ranges can be traced on the continents even when erosion has reduced high peaks to low rounded hills. The ancient Caledonian Mountains which run through Norway and Sweden (Kjolen Mts), Scotland (Grampian Mts) and the south-east USA (Appalachian Mts) must have been as high as the Alps in the Devonian Period when they first arose, 400 million years ago. Tracks of these ancient ranges give us valuable clues to the position of ancient oceans.

Geologists can find out the age of various rocks, when the rocks were folded and metamorphosed, and when the range was uplifted. Strangely the uplift often turns out to be many millions of years later than the folding, though by the plate tectonic theory the two should happen together.

The Alps were raised 20 million years ago as Africa pushed northwards into Europe. Even while the mountains were still forming the forces of erosion started to gnaw away at the rocks, attempting to level them. This valley was carved by a glacier during the Ice Age, half a million years ago.

Deserts and Ice Fields

One-fifth of the land is covered by desert—areas which have less than 25 cm (10 in) of rain each year. The largest deserts are the Sahara which covers much of northern Africa, the Central Australian desert, the deserts of California and Arizona, and Saudi Arabia, Iran, and Afghanistan. The driest desert in the world is the Atacama in Chile where there was no rain for 400 years up to 1971.

We generally think of deserts as hot. The highest shade temperature ever recorded is 58°C (136°F) in the northern Sahara, while Dallol in Ethiopia has the highest average annual temperature, 34°C (94°F). But even in hot deserts, clear skies and barren rock surfaces mean that temperatures often fall below freezing at night. Cold deserts are found high up in mountain ranges, such as the Atacama Desert in Chile, and in Mongolia, central Asia.

Where there is no water nothing can live. Most deserts have some rain and also oases where water-bearing rocks come to the surface. Cacti are plants that have adapted to the desert. They store water in their bulbous stems, having a network of roots just below the ground to catch every drop of rain and dew, and they dispense with leaves to avoid losing water by evaporation. Other plants grow fast and flower when it does rain, producing tough seeds which lie dormant in the ground, maybe for years, until the next shower. Desert animals are the camel, desert rat, desert fox, rattlesnake and scorpion. Many of these live underground and have special mechanisms for conserving water.

Many deserts go for years without rain and then enjoy a tremendous downpour when several centimetres often fall in a few hours. This water quickly runs away and

evaporates, so that after a short time the land is as dry as before.

We usually think of deserts as sandy. In fact only about one-fifth of the world's desert area is made up of rolling dunes of sand, the remainder is either bare rock with occasional patches of sand, or a stony surface of rubble, gravel or pebbles.

By studying today's deserts, geologists can tell that certain rocks formed in deserts. Most geological periods had some deserts, but about 250 million years ago deserts covered much of Britain, southern Europe, North America, and North Africa. This period, the Permian, was a true 'desert age'.

Ice Fields The only two extensive ice sheets today cover Antarctica at the South Pole, and Greenland in the north. Here the average temperature in the warmest month

is less than 10°C (50°F) and less than −3°C (26·5°F) in the coldest. Most of these areas are within the Arctic and Antarctic Circles where the Sun never rises during winter and never sets in summer. Other smaller ice-caps are found above the snowline in high mountain ranges, such as the Himalayas, Canadian Rockies and Andes. Around the North Pole the sea is frozen to a great depth.

Low temperature alone will not form an ice sheet. Northern Siberia is one of the coldest places on Earth, but there is so little snow that it melts each year in the brief summer. As soon as slightly more snow falls each year than melts, a snow field begins to grow, making the whole area colder as it does so. As it builds up, the soft snow at the bottom is compressed to form ice by the weight above and eventually

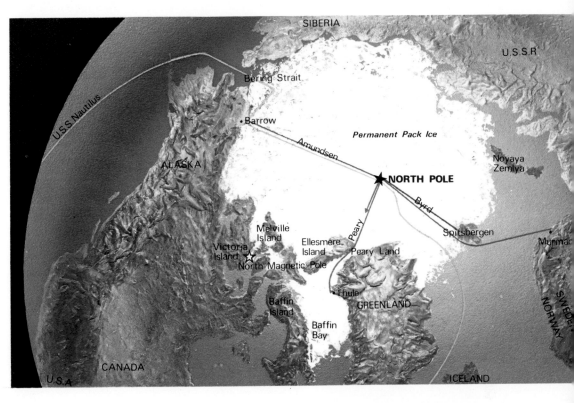

Left The desert plains of central Australia, showing the very sparse vegetation and the thin, sandy soil. The hills in the distance, the Olgas, are typical of the very steep-sided, rounded hills that form in deserts.

Right The ice fields of the North Pole, showing the routes taken by some of the early explorers. An American, Robert Peary, was the first man to reach the North Pole, in 1909. The South Pole was conquered in 1911 by Roald Amundsen. Also marked on the map is the present position of the North Magnetic Pole.

Below right The Antarctic ice sheet, showing pressure ridges pushed up by the moving ice.

begins to spread outwards from the cold centre in a series of tongues called glaciers. Every ice sheet has a central zone where snow falls and ice builds up, and an outer edge where glaciers carry ice away to melt or break off into the sea or lakes. The weight of a thick ice sheet is so enormous that it pushes the land surface down. Greenland may well have been a mountainous land before the ice developed, but much of its land surface is now well below sea-level.

Ice flows off Antarctica in great sheets, breaking up at the sea to form huge flat icebergs. The Greenland ice sheet, as well as the smaller mountain sheets, gives rise to numerous valley glaciers which flow downhill at speeds of one metre (3 ft) or so each day. The ice flows faster in the centre of the glacier than at the sides and faster on the outside of bends than on the inside. Deep cracks or 'crevasses' open on the surface of the glacier, and on warm days there may be pools of water. As the ice moves it scrapes pieces of rock from the valley sides and floor, carries them downhill, and drops them where the ice is melting. The

pile of rock, sand and gravel is called a moraine. Ice in a glacier always flows downhill, but when it melts faster than the snow falls, the glacier will appear to retreat up the valley. In most areas of the world glaciers have retreated during the present century.

Few, if any, animals or plants live on the ice itself, though lichen and small plants appear in summer, wherever a patch of rock or soil is exposed. The Arctic and Antarctic seas are rich in fish, which are hunted by polar bears, seals and penguins. Apart from the Eskimos in the north, the first human hunters to visit the Poles came in search of whales. Nowadays there are permanent colonies of scientists in Antarctica and around the Arctic.

By the shapes of their mountain valleys and by the presence of ancient moraines many areas show they were once covered by ice. During the last million years the ice has spread and then retreated many times, and the period is known as the great Ice Age of the Pleistocene. Preserved in the rocks are traces of many more ancient ice ages over the last thousand million years.

Climate

The average weather conditions of an area, measured over a period of years, is the climate. Temperature, rain and snowfall, wind, and the amount of water vapour in the air (humidity) all play a part. Climate determines animal and plant life, and affects the geological processes of rock weathering and erosion.

Among the many factors which govern climate are latitude, hilliness, and nearness to the sea. The Sun is strongest, and therefore the temperature highest, when it is directly overhead, and weakest when its rays pass through a great thickness of atmosphere and strike the ground obliquely. This results in a tropical zone around the Equator, two temperate zones in the middle latitudes, and two polar zones. This overall temperature difference on the globe sets up a pattern of winds

which in turn affect the climate. At the Equator warm air rises so that the 'trade winds' blow in from the north and south. The warm equatorial air cools as it rises and sinks in the middle latitudes, causing steady cool winds to blow north and south towards the Poles. These winds do not in fact blow directly north and south, but are deflected by the spin of the Earth. The trade winds blow north east and south east, the cool winds (the 'westerlies') blow north west and south west. These winds set up slow but steady water currents in the oceans of the northern hemisphere, carrying warm water up the east coast of North America, across the north Atlantic to Britain and Scandinavia, and similarly up the western edge of the Pacific. Cold water returns past Spain and West Africa

and also past California. In the southern hemisphere the general circulation is anti-clockwise.

In any area temperature decreases as one climbs a hill or mountain—a drop of about 7 deg C (13 deg F) for every 1,000 metres (3,000 ft). This is because the thinner atmosphere at high altitude traps the Sun's warmth less effectively. Mountains and hills also affect the rainfall around them. At any temperature air can carry a certain amount of water vapour, and this amount is greater the higher the temperature. Warm air blowing across the sea picks up all the water vapour it can carry. If on reaching land it rises up over a range of hills, it will cool and clouds of tiny water droplets or ice crystals will form. The droplets or crystals grow in size and fall as rain or snow

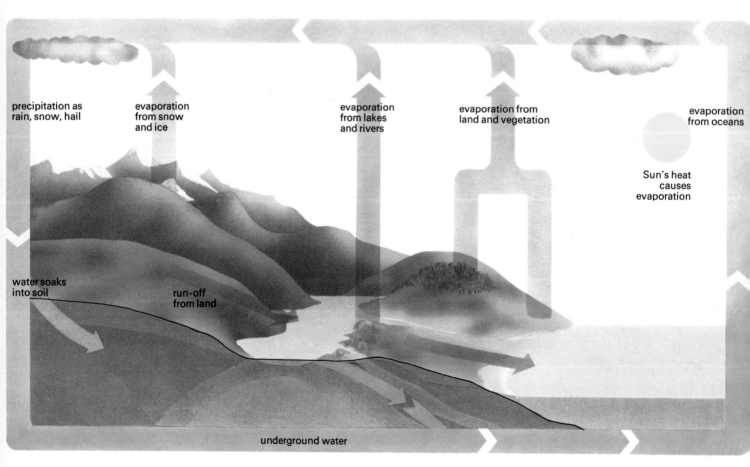

precipitation as rain, snow, hail

evaporation from snow and ice

evaporation from lakes and rivers

evaporation from land and vegetation

evaporation from oceans

Sun's heat causes evaporation

water soaks into soil

run-off from land

underground water

on the slopes of the hills. Beyond the hills may be an area where rain rarely falls, perhaps even a desert.

In tropical areas rain falls every afternoon in a great thunderstorm. The land heats up in the morning and air laden with water vapour rises. Clouds form in the early afternoon, and about 4 o'clock it rains for an hour. Lightning is an electric spark which flashes between clouds or from one cloud to the ground. Thunder is the sound wave set up by the sudden blast of heat in the spark. Lightning is seen before thunder is heard because light travels faster than sound. The number of seconds from the flash to the rumble is approximately the number of miles you are from the centre of the storm (1 mile = 1·6 km).

The third influence on climate is distance from the sea. Land areas heat and cool faster than the sea.

During the day wind blows inland from the sea as the Sun warms the land; at night wind blows offshore as the land cools. At the end of the summer the sea keeps some warmth and moderates the effect of winter, and in the spring it is cool and slows the onset of summer. Extreme climates often develop in central areas of large continents, making them very hot in summer and icy cold in winter.

Below left The water cycle. The total amount of water on the Earth doesn't alter, but it is continually changing its form and position as the temperature changes.

Below A map showing the different climates of the world. The very simple pattern that would be predicted on the basis of distance from the Equator is almost hidden by the influence of other factors described in the text.

climatic regions

	tropical forest	continually hot ; heavy rainfall throughout year
	savanna	hot summers, warm winters ; wet in summer
	tropical steppe	continually hot ; little rainfall
	continental steppe	warm summers, cold winters ; little precipitation
	tropical desert	continually hot ; little rainfall
	continental desert	hot summers, cold winters ; little precipitation
	subtropical	hot summers, mild winters ; moderate precipitation
	temperate	warm summers, cool winters ; moderate precipitation
	subarctic	short cool summers, long cold winters ; little precipitation
	tundra	short cold summers, long very cold winters ; little precipitation
	highland	cooler than surrounding areas
	icecap	continually cold ; little precipitation

Part 2
GEOLOGICAL PROCESSES AT WORK

The Weathering of Rock

As soon as a rock appears on the surface of the Earth, and sometimes even before, it is under attack. It may crack up, be worn away to dust, or it may dissolve. Some tough rocks can survive on the Earth's surface for a very long time, but they are all destroyed in the end. Most rocks are formed deep underground, many of them at high temperatures, so it is not surprising that they are unstable when exposed on a mountain slope or a cliff face. The changes produced in

Cracking is one form of mechanical weathering. Although rocks form underground in solid masses, rocks at the surface are almost always cut by sets of regularly spaced cracks, or joints. These are caused by stress set up as the rock moves underground, and by the decrease of pressure as the rock comes close to the surface. Once the rock is exposed, temperature changes cause further cracking. We have seen that both in hot deserts and polar regions there can be rapid changes

of temperature which cause stones to expand and contract in their surface layers, setting up stresses which may break them. A cracked or porous stone that is wet will break when it freezes because the water trapped in the stone expands with great force when it turns to ice.

rocks by this attack are collectively known as 'weathering'—rather a misleading term as only some of the changes are caused by weather as we normally think of it.

Weathering is of two types, mechanical and chemical. The first breaks up a rock into smaller and smaller pieces, or wears away its softest components, without altering its make-up; the second alters the composition of minerals in the rock by chemical reaction with materials at the Earth's surface. The altered minerals are usually softer than the original ones and so quickly disintegrate. The two types of weathering are closely linked and often hard to distinguish.

Top left Mechanical weathering by temperature change in the Sahara Desert, Algeria. The sandstone cliffs are being broken down to small rocks and finally to sand.

Previous page Ocean waves—a reminder of the power of water in wearing away the land.

Top right Mechanical weathering by wind and sand in Goblin Valley, Utah, USA. The soft lower layers are being worn away faster than the harder cap rock.

Above Chemical weathering has converted the felspar in this granite to clay. A high-pressure hose is being used to wash out the clay, which is used for potting. St Austell, Cornwall, UK.

This is known as 'frost-wedging'. Growing plants can break up large boulders by the force of their roots entering and growing inside a cracked or porous stone, or when a large slab of rock rests over a growing shoot which, as it grows upwards, will find the smallest crack and penetrate this, causing a gradual widening.

Another important type of mechanical weathering is abrasion, the wearing away of rock by repeated small impacts, each of which removes a tiny amount of material as dust or small grains. Wind does not abrade, but wind carrying particles of sand can wear away rock in no time, carving layered outcrops into fantastic shapes. Similarly, flowing water does not abrade on its own, but when it is carrying pebbles, gravel and sand, rock outcrops will be broken up and worn away. As this happens of course the pebbles and gravel will themselves be abraded. The ice of a glacier does not abrade very much, but the stones and boulders carried along by the glacier will act on rock outcrops like a gigantic rasp.

Chemical weathering is largely carried out by rain and stream water. This is not chemically pure (H_2O) but contains carbon dioxide from the atmosphere which makes it a very dilute and weak acid (H_2CO_3). Acids react with carbonates to form soluble salts called bicarbonates, and by this reaction rainwater slowly dissolves limestone, marble and chalk, and attacks the calcium carbonate that cements the grains of a sandstone together. Felspar, a mineral common in igneous rocks like granite and basalt, reacts very slowly with rainwater to give soft powdery minerals called clays. Other minerals in igneous rocks that weather in a similar way are augite, biotite and olivine. When the water contains traces of organic compounds from the soil, and particularly acids from rotting vegetation, it acts more powerfully. Like all chemical reactions, these proceed faster at high temperatures than low.

A layer of broken rock fragments will generally be colonized by bacteria, lichens and mosses. As they die and decay, moulds and humus begin to accumulate and soon ferns and grasses will grow. Eventually a soil will be formed which will support shrubs and even trees. Soil is the product of decay, but it is the medium of growth for plants, and thus of life for animals. A layer of rich fertile soil takes a long time to develop and should be treated with respect. When a deep pit is dug the soil is seen to consist of a number of distinct layers. At the top is the rich humus layer, second comes the main topsoil layer through which water passes, removing soluble matter; third is the subsoil in which this soluble matter is being deposited, and fourth is a layer of weathered rock fragments. Factors which affect the character of soil are climate, bedrock, hilliness and the length of time the soil has been developing.

People can affect soils in many ways. All too often they have thoughtlessly cut down trees or allowed sheep to destroy grasslands, leaving the soil unprotected from rain and wind. Vast areas of the USA and central Africa were turned into dust deserts within a few years of this sort of treatment. Soil developed on clay is cold and heavy—we add sand or lime to lighten it; soil on sand is light and will not hold water—we add humus to enrich it. Chemical fertilizers are often added to increase the power of a soil to produce a particular crop, or to replace materials taken from the soil during intensive farming. More and more, especially among the very technologically-advanced countries of the Western world, chemicals of various kinds are being used to improve land and fight pests and disease.

Right Five important types of soil developed under different weather conditions are shown.

rain forest—red and yellow laterite

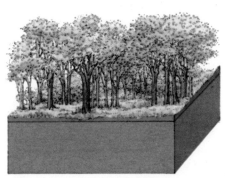
forest—red and yellow podzols

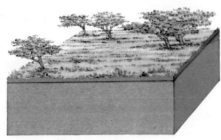
savanna—brown podzols

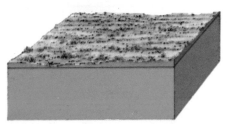
steppe—brown chernozems

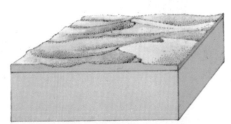
desert—grey and red desert

The Work of Water

Weathering would be of small account were it not for the various transporting agents that remove the weathered material, exposing the fresh surface underneath. These agents are water, ice and wind; the driving force behind them is gravity.

On its own, gravity is responsible for many small, but nevertheless spectacular, movements of weathered rock. Rockfalls from cliffs, avalanches in mountains, landslides in areas of soft sediment, and mudflows in areas of high rainfall are examples. These events can be disastrous in human terms. In one landslide triggered off by an earthquake in Kansu Province, China, in 1920, 200,000 people died. In contrast is the slow downhill movement of soil and vegetation on any slope that is called 'creep'. This shows up in the way poles and old fences lean over, roads crack, and

gravestones tumble. A cut into the land often shows layers of rock at the surface bent in the downslope direction. This creep is speeded up in areas which frequently freeze and then thaw, and for this reason slopes are very low in such places.

The most important agent that transports weathered rock, and in the process continues its weathering, is running water. Next time you are in hilly country sit down and watch a small river or stream. As the water bubbles along, rock particles are on the move. Pebbles are rolling or sliding on the river bed, and smaller fragments are moving downhill in long jumps. Up above the bed the water flow is turbulent, with eddies carrying sand and mineral grains in suspension. The water may be clear, but now and again a tiny landslip drops soil in from the bank, making a muddy streak in the water. Two things you

cannot see are that there are chemicals dissolved from the rocks on the hilltop being carried in solution by the water, and that whenever one pebble or sand grain bumps into another a tiny piece may be knocked off. In the thirty minutes you watch maybe a cupful of weathered rock is moved a few metres. It is not much, but in time this stream will wear the whole hill away. If you return after a heavy storm the stream will be in flood and will be moving great boulders. Then you will realize that the hill cannot survive for ever.

Further downstream our river will be wider and slower, and will be flowing down an open valley. The bed of the river is made of pebbles, but they only move after a storm; there are no boulders to be seen. Sand and mineral grains still dance in the turbulent waters, rock fragments roll and jump along the

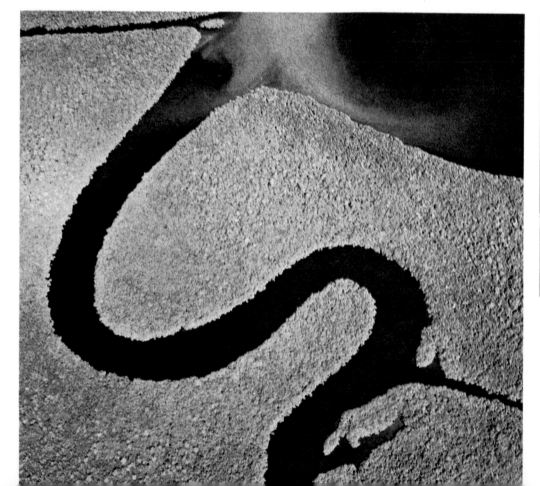

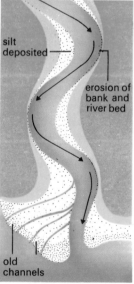

silt deposited

erosion of bank and river bed

old channels

Left A senile river meandering through a heavily forested plain. The water moves slowly and only carries fine-grained and dissolved material.

Above A diagram showing how a meandering river constantly changes its course by erosion and deposition on its banks.

representing an average lowering of the land by 1 m in 9,000 years.

While rivers are the sculptors of the surface of the land, the sea nibbles away at its edges. Wherever the land rises or sea-level falls, a line of cliffs forms along the sea-shore, and these are attacked by the waves. The force of a large breaking wave is tremendous, easily opening cracks and crevices in the toughest rock. Sea caves, natural arches, stacks and wave-cut platforms are all formed this way.

Top left The San Juan River, USA, has cut deeply into an ancient plain through its rejuvenation. This deep canyon is the result.

bottom, and the dissolved chemicals are still there. The rock fragments and sand grains are somewhat rounder than when you first saw them, having had their corners knocked off in all the jumping and bumping. In thirty minutes this river might move a bucketful of weathered rock. As well as carrying it, it is also wearing it away. The wide valley was formed by the river digging downwards to form a narrow gorge, and rockfalls, landslides and creep opening it out into its present form.

Still further towards the sea, our river will be very wide, meandering slowly across an open plain. The river bed is sandy, and grains roll or jump along. Flow in the river is smoother and there are few eddies. Clays and dissolved matter, as well as leaves and twigs, move out to sea. There is little erosion happening on the river bed, but wherever the river bends the outer bank is being worn away and its course is constantly changing. At different times it has flowed all over this wide plain. In half an hour this river might transport a lorryload of fine weathered rock material.

As our river ends in the sea, so it is tending to erode the land down to sea-level. The higher above this level it is, the more power it has to erode and transport. If it is undisturbed it will work slower and slower as it wears away the hills, and will end up close to sea-level, its work nearly completed. For this reason our mountain stream is called 'youthful'—just starting its work —the middle reaches 'mature', and the final stage 'senile'.

Movement of the Earth's crust, rise or fall of sea-level, or a change of climate can interrupt this life history and can rejuvenate an old stream, causing it to dig deeply down into its flat plain, or can age a river, causing it to fill up its valley with sand and gravel.

It has been estimated that the world's major rivers transport 8,000 million tonnes of rock debris from the land into the sea, about one-third of it in solution, in a year,

Above The magnificent Victoria Falls on the Zambezi River mark the border between Zambia and Zimbabwe Rhodesia.

Below The four stages in the life of a river. As the river ages it becomes wider and more meandering.

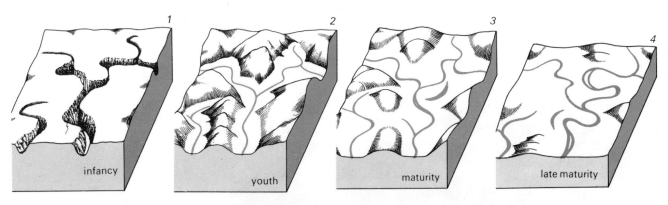

infancy   youth   maturity   late maturity

Rivers that Disappear

We have seen that water containing carbon dioxide is weakly acidic and will therefore react with calcium carbonate, the main constituent of limestone, to produce a soluble salt. There are many areas of the world where the surface is made entirely of limestone, and where rivers behave in a rather strange way. Limestone, like many other rocks, is cut by joints running in a number of fixed directions. Rain falling on a limestone plateau runs down through these joints until it comes to an impervious layer through which it cannot pass. This may mark the base of the limestone or may be a shale within it. The water then follows this impervious layer just as if it were the ground surface, until eventually it emerges into the open air. Once a drainage path through the limestone is established, then the chemical reactions begin which weather away the rock. There are no surface streams on limestone plateaux.

The narrow joints down which the water seeps are quickly opened out into fissures by the action of the water, and may have their sides furrowed and fluted. The underground stream established down below will dissolve out a tunnel for itself and may develop lakes, rapids and waterfalls, just like those on the surface. Long-continued chemical action, together with underground rockfalls, will in time produce a labyrinth of intercommunicating caverns, tunnels, chasms and shafts. However long and complicated its underground path, eventually the river will emerge

Left A limestone pavement in Yorkshire, England. The open fissures where rainwater has opened out narrow joints can be seen.

Above A close-up view of stalactites showing drops of water, each leaving a tiny deposit of calcium carbonate.

Top right A speleologist admiring a fine group of cave pillars, stalactites and stalagmites.

into the open air to continue its journey to the sea.

Cave explorers (speleologists) risk their lives to trace these underground rivers and to explore and map the fantastic cave systems that result. The largest system in the world is under the Mammoth Cave National Park in Kentucky, USA, which has a total mapped passageway length of 231 km (144 miles). The largest known single cavern is the Big Room of the Carlsbad Caverns in New Mexico, USA, which is 1,300 m (4,270 ft) long and reaches a height of 100 m (328 ft). Carlsbad Caverns were discovered in 1901 when a cowboy noticed a huge flock of bats flying out of a small hole in the ground.

In addition to the underground rivers there is generally a slow seepage of lime-charged water down through joints and crevices in the rock. As water drips through the rock or down the walls of caves, so tiny amounts of calcium carbonate are redeposited. When the drop lands on the floor of the cave some more comes out of solution. In time long icicle-like pendants called stalactites grow downwards from the rock, and thicker columns, called stalagmites, build up from the floor. In time stalactites and stalagmites unite to become pillars, and many extraordinary shapes can form, often given fanciful names by commercially-minded cave-owners. Where water trickles out continuously from a long roof joint, or where it runs down a sloping wall, a sheet of encrusted calcium carbonate may form.

Although few of us will ever explore caves underground, there are many interesting surface features in limestone areas. Soil is usually rather thin so there are many rock outcrops. In dry areas the soil is made up largely of a red clay which is an insoluble residue left behind when limestone dissolves. There is little mechanical weathering in these areas, so the soil contains few stones. In high plateaux a limestone pavement may develop showing

the open fissures developed along the joints. Where the surface contours concentrate the water running into a limestone system, a large funnel, or 'swallow hole',

may form. Gaping Ghyll, in Yorkshire, England, is a swallow hole 120 m (362 ft) deep into which a small stream disappears. Some streams appear and disappear several times during their course. Others flow partly above and partly below ground, so they seem to disappear during dry weather. Rockfalls underground often produce depressions on the surface known as 'sink holes'. Massive rockfalls along an underground stream system may open the river to the sky and leave it running along a steep-sided canyon whose floor is made up of tumbled blocks. Cheddar Gorge in Somerset, England, is one famous example, though here the river has since changed its course and the gorge is now dry.

Limestone regions showing these features are said to display a 'karst' topography, the name coming from a plateau in northern Yugoslavia.

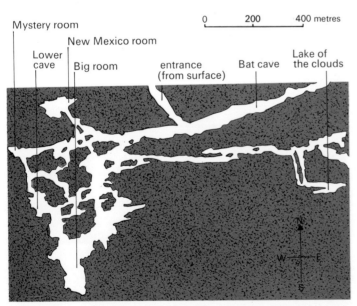

Mystery room
New Mexico room
Lower cave
Big room
entrance (from surface)
Bat cave
Lake of the clouds

0   200   400 metres

A map of the Carlsbad Caverns in New Mexico, USA, giving some idea of the complexity of a large cave system. Chemical weathering must have gone on for millions of years to remove such a vast quantity of limestone.

The Work of Wind and Ice

In certain areas wind and ice are as important as water in carrying sediment.

Rock outcrops in a desert weather mechanically into broken fragments, grains and dust. Few plants will grow in the very dry conditions, so there is no layer of soil. The wind works in such an environment by deflation (blowing away) and abrasion (wearing away). Deflation is simply the picking up and carrying away of loose particles. Dust and silt are picked up by the wind and carried high into the air. Sand grains turn over and jump across the surface, while small pebbles are rolled along. Large stones and boulders are left standing on their own. Deflation gradually lowers the desert surface until there is a continuous layer of stones and boulders. In semi-arid regions where there is a thin layer of soil, deflation works in patches. If the grass dies in one place the wind will pick away at the soil and sand and will soon form a shallow wind-scoured basin. Grass on the

edges of this basin will die, and soon the whole area will be a desert. Abrasion is part of the process of rock weathering (see page 35).

Very cold, glaciated regions are similar to deserts in many ways. Weathering is mainly mechanical, there is little soil, and little running water. Glaciers, like the wind, weather away rock as well as carrying it. They act as ploughs, files and sledges, all in one. As ploughs they scrape up loose rock fragments and gouge out blocks of bedrock; as files they rasp away at projecting rock masses in their path; as sledges they carry the debris, together with rock waste fallen from overhanging cliffs, down into warmer regions. As a carrying agent ice differs from both wind and water. It can carry material at its sides and top as well

Above The head of the Aletsch Glacier, Switzerland, showing the four great cirques from which it originated. The ridges between the cirques are called 'arêtes'.

Above left Further down the Aletsch Glacier we see the dark stripes of debris being carried by the ice.

Left Sand grains blown along by the wind in the Sahara Desert, Africa.

as underneath it; it can carry very large and very small pieces of rock side by side; the rocks it carries do not bump against each other and so do not become rounded.

Glaciers exert an enormous effect on the landscape. Those which are not run-offs from a huge ice sheet start their journeys from steep-walled bowls close to the mountain peaks, called 'cirques'. The bowl begins to form by frost-wedging as a snowbank builds up, and is enlarged as bedrock is plucked away when the snow is compressed into ice and the glacier begins to flow. A newly formed glacier generally follows a river valley. The ploughing and filing described above widen this at the bottom until it has a U-shaped cross-section, rather than the original V-shape. The floor and sides of the valley will be scraped clean of any soil or soft weathered rock, and will be polished and scratched by the passage of the ice and its boulders.

Laying Down the Debris

We have seen how rock outcrops are weathered and how the debris is transported. We now look at the ways the debris, or sediment, is laid down, or deposited.

Particles of sediment carried along by water will be deposited when the flow slows down and they can no longer be supported. Larger particles need more rapid flow to keep them moving than smaller ones, so in general coarse grains are dropped before fine ones. This means that water-laid deposits tend to be 'sorted', containing particles within a narrow range of sizes. Because river transport involves bumping and bouncing, the particles tend to be rounded. Particles carried by a stream or river will be deposited and picked up many times as the water changes its speed. They may stay for thousands of years on the floor of a lake or in a deserted channel, but each time they move it is down towards the sea, and that is where most of them end up. When a river carrying sediment reaches the sea its flow

Above Enormous sand dunes with wind-rippled surfaces in the Sahara Desert, Africa.

Below The flood plain built up by debris deposited by the Athabaska River, Canada. A small triangular delta is visible where the river enters the sea.

is checked and the coarse particles will be deposited provided the waves and sea currents are not strong enough to carry them on further. Where the waves and currents are weak the river tends to build out a delta of sand and silt. The River Nile has a triangular delta 250 km (150 miles) across, while the Mississippi has a vast irregular delta shaped like a bird's foot, about the same size as the Nile delta.

Waves and currents carry sediment from the land along the shore (longshore drift) to build up the spits, bars and banks that are found in many areas, or else out to sea where it is laid down in flat sheets on the floor of the continental shelf. These sheets of sediment are well sorted and are generally sand or mud; gravel and pebbles are rarely carried out to sea. Mixed with the sediment will be the bones and shells of underwater creatures. A tiny amount of the very finest material is swept right off the shelf and carried on down to the deep ocean floor.

Material carried out to sea in solution—principally calcium carbonate—is used by invertebrate animals like corals, clams and sea urchins to build their skeletons. In other areas marine algae can trap growing crystals of calcium carbonate and build up enormous banks and reefs of the material. The Bahamas is the classic area for this type of deposition.

Sediment dropped from melting ice is not sorted but contains boulders, stones, pebbles, sand and clay all mixed together; the particles are not rounded but are jagged and broken; the sediment does not occur in flat layers. A valley glacier which stays the same size for many centuries will build up a huge pile, or moraine, of this sediment, which is known as 'boulder clay', at its nose, where the ice is melting. If the glacier is either advancing or retreating, a similar moraine will be built up wherever a certain position is held for a while. As the ice melts, rivers form which carry away much of the finer sediment down towards the sea. Eventually all that is left of a moraine will be a small number of very large boulders, some of them carried hundreds of kilometres by the ice. These rather 'out of place' boulders are known as erratics.

Wind-laid deposits are usually extremely well sorted; composed of very well-rounded grains; not laid down in perfectly flat sheets, and are never coarser than sand. Sand carried by the wind builds up as rippled sheets, or as huge wave-like

dunes having a gentle slope to windward and a steeper slope to the lee. Sand sheets and dune fields stay on the move until a change in wind pattern or rainfall stops them and they have a chance of permanent preservation. Dust lifted by the wind is often carried hundreds of kilometres away from the deserts and laid down as thick sheets of yellow or buff sediment which is called loess.

Above Piles of boulder clay accumulating around a melting glacier in Alaska.

Below Sand forms on a beach as small particles of rock are worn down through friction with each other and through being buffeted by moving water. Fine grains settle on slopes and heavier, coarse grains on more level areas.

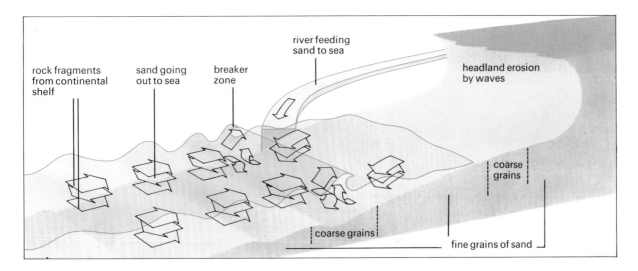

rock fragments from continental shelf

sand going out to sea

breaker zone

river feeding sand to sea

headland erosion by waves

coarse grains

coarse grains

fine grains of sand

Turning Debris into Rock

Almost as soon as the particles of sediment are deposited on the sea-floor, further particles will be swept over them, and in no time they will be buried. As the depth of burial increases a number of changes take place in the soft sediment which eventually turn it into a hard rock. The main changes come about by pressure and the arrival of a cementing mineral.

A pure quartz sandstone will not be affected by pressure alone, even of deep burial, but will be turned into rock as minerals, like calcium carbonate or silica, crystallize when seawater saturates the sandstone. This may happen soon after burial or not at all; near Leningrad, in the USSR, lies a sand 500 million years old that is hardly cemented at all. Silt and mud are more often affected by pressure which squeezes water out of the sediment, leaving a soft, rather flaky rock called shale, than by the growth of calcite which would result in a rather hard calcareous mudstone. Lime deposits harden quite suddenly into limestone as water is forced out of them.

These various processes of rock formation tend to emphasize the minute differences in composition in the layers of the sediment, and to produce a rock which is conspicuously banded. This banding is known as stratification and the individual bands as strata.

Many other chemical changes may take place in a sediment during the time that it is buried. A limestone, for example, may be affected by magnesium-rich water and turn into the magnesium carbonate rock, dolomite. Similarly, mudstones and shales may be phosphatized; limestone may be replaced by silica or by iron minerals, and black shales may develop the mineral iron pyrite. These processes, collectively called metasomatism, greatly increase the variety of rock found on the Earth's surface.

When sediment is carried down to great depths in the crust then more profound changes take place that are known as metamorphism, caused by the great pressures and high temperatures involved. The sediments lose their original character and are known as metamorphic rocks. It is often difficult to be sure just what a metamorphic rock originally was.

Quartz sandstone is relatively little affected by even severe metamorphism, the quartz grains merely locking tighter together with the removal of some of the calcite cement. A mudstone or shale is first squeezed quite flat by metamorphism and all flaky minerals

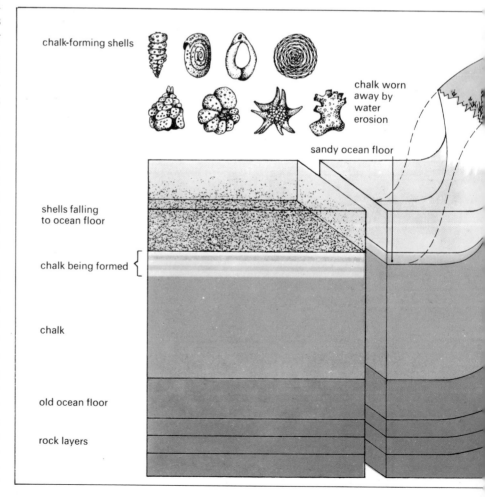

chalk-forming shells

chalk worn away by water erosion

sandy ocean floor

shells falling to ocean floor

chalk being formed

chalk

old ocean floor

rock layers

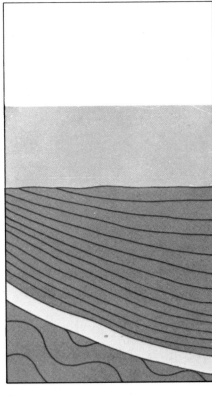

water ☐
mud ■
sand ☐

flattened mud ■
mineral ▦
sand ☐

1

2

3

Top left An outcrop of the igneous rock, granite, on Dartmoor, England. This mass of granite was at a temperature of 700°C (1500°F) when it pushed up into the slates which surround it, and produced a zone of metamorphic rock 2 km (1 mile) wide.

Left Chalk is made of the shells of tiny sea creatures. Gradually the shells of the dead animals build up on the sandy ocean bed. The movement of the seas covers these with sand and the weight of the sand and water above presses the shells until they become chalk.

Above **1)** a bed of well-rounded, well-sorted quartz sand with a few shell fragments being laid down from a slow-flowing river close to the sea; **2)** the same bed buried under several hundred metres of other sediment and thus under great pressure. Calcite begins to crystalize in the spaces between the grains; **3)** the same bed transformed into rock and outcropping in a mountainous region.

Right Sheer cliffs of metamorphic rocks in Norway, once muds and now hard, splintery slates and schists.

arranged at right angles to the direction of squeeze. This gives the well-known rock, slate. With a higher temperature grains of the flaky mineral mica begin to grow alongside the original minerals, giving the banded and glittery rock called schist. Still higher temperatures and pressures result in a rock called gneiss, in which white or pink bands of felspar and white quartz alternate with bands of black mica. One would hardly suspect that this rock was metamorphosed mud. Limestone recrystallizes when it is deeply buried; original features such as stratification and fossil shells disappear and a very even-grained rock called marble forms.

In metamorphism heat and pressure usually act together, but occasionally one is present without the other. When a body of molten rock is intruded among the rocks of the Earth's crust, there will be very strong heat but little pressure. A small body of molten rock may have a band of metamorphic rock a few metres wide, while a large

granite intrusion may be surrounded for several kilometres by metamorphics. The typical rock formed in this situation is called a hornfels. It is very hard and compact and shows no signs of banding.

45

Uplift, Folds and Faults

Over the last few sections we have reviewed the destructive processes that are gnawing away the land, yet the hills and mountains to be found all over the world show us that there must be some constructive power at work which repairs the damage of erosion. What are the forces that raise our sedimentary or metamorphic rock from a position a kilometre or more below the seafloor up into the peaks of a mountain range like the Andes or Himalayas?

The forces are those that move the plates of the Earth. We have already seen on page 20 how plate collisions and undercuttings raise up mountain chains from the bottom of the sea. These are the forces that provide the heat and pressure for metamorphism, that bend and break the once flat layers of rock, and that are responsible for earthquakes and volcanoes wherever they occur.

In stable regions of the Earth's crust sedimentary rocks will stay more or less horizontal and will be gently raised up to form one of the great low-lying plateaux of the land. In unstable areas the rocks will be folded, squeezed and broken before or during their uplift. Folds can be anything from an enormous arch of rock many kilo-

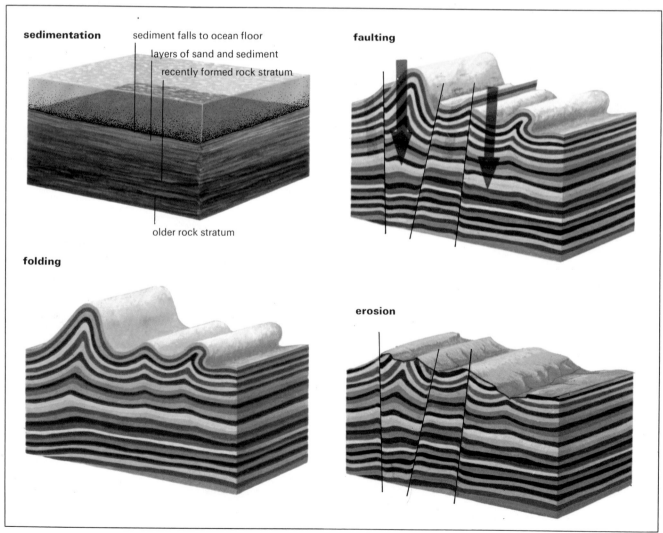

sedimentation

sediment falls to ocean floor

layers of sand and sediment

recently formed rock stratum

older rock stratum

faulting

folding

erosion

metres across to a series of tiny crinkles on the surface of a slate. They can be seen in cliff faces in mountainous areas and often in boulders in a river or on the sea-shore. Faults again range from the great fractures which mark the boundaries of the plates of the Earth's crust, like the San Andreas Fault in California, to tiny breaks within a single crystal which are studied by geologists, but which do not have the disruptive potential of their giant brothers.

There are some types of uplift and folding that are nothing to do with plate movement. At the present time much of Canada and the northern USA is rising up at the rate of about 1 cm ($\frac{1}{2}$ in) each year, an effect of the last ice age when a thick ice-cap forced these areas of crust down into the mantle. The ice has gone and the land is still rising to compensate. Whenever a mass of rather light and fluid material rises up to the surface of the Earth it is bound to fold and fault the surrounding rock strata. This happens when a body of granite rises up, and just the same thing can happen with salt and mud. Under these special circumstances huge and complex fold structures are formed that have a purely local cause, unrelated to the plate structure of the Earth.

Now that our sedimentary or metamorphic rocks are exposed at the Earth's surface, we have reached the point we started at on page 20, and the 'rock cycle' is complete. For thousands of millions of years the material that makes up the crust of the Earth has been involved in a constant cycle of weathering – erosion – sedimentation – rock formation – uplift – weathering. The same cycle will continue as long as the Earth endures. The best demonstration of the reality of the rock cycle comes in the structures known as unconformities. Here ancient folded rocks are cut across by a plane of erosion, showing they must have been uplifted, and overlain by flat-lying marine sediments which indicates in turn that they must have subsided under the sea again. The fact that these structures are visible shows that, once again, they have been uplifted in a constant process of movement.

Opposite top left Folds in metamorphic rock formed when the rock was hot and under great pressure deep underground. Under these conditions rock does not crack but bends and even flows.

Opposite bottom left Diagrams showing the formation of folds and faults in surface layers of rock, and their subsequent erosion.

Above An unconformity exposed at Kerrera, Scotland.

Below The rock cycle: a diagram showing how the three main classes of rock are related to each other, and how each may be affected by uplift, weathering and erosion.

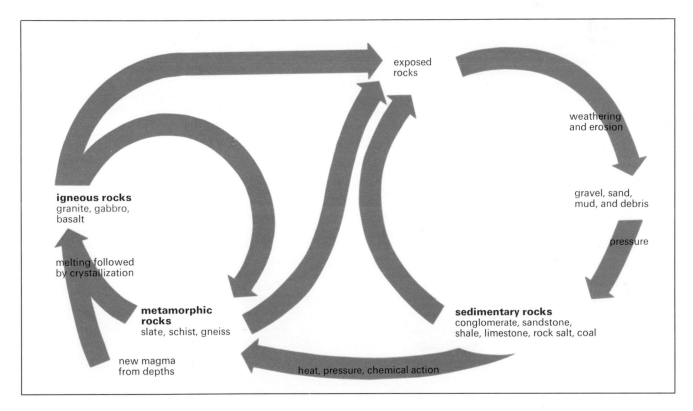

Earthquakes

An earthquake is the shaking of the land that occurs when rocks suddenly move along a fault deep underground. Three sorts of shock waves, called 'push-pull', 'shake' and 'long' waves, travel through the Earth from the place where the movement took place, getting weaker all the time.

Earthquakes mostly occur along the great unstable lines where plates are forming or disappearing. The mid-ocean ridges, deep ocean trenches and island arcs, and growing mountain ranges are the main sites of earthquakes. Hundreds of thousands happen each year, most of them very small or in uninhabited areas. Occasionally a severe earthquake hits a city and the results are disastrous.

The Lisbon earthquake of 1755 is among the most famous and terrible. Three shocks came at intervals of forty minutes, the first destroying most of the large buildings and starting innumerable fires. Loss of life was very heavy as, being All Saints Day, the churches were crowded with worshippers, several

of whom were crushed to death. Many people fled down to the harbours and quays for safety, there to be drowned by a great tidal wave, or 'tsunami', set off by an underwater earthquake.

Another terrible event was the San Francisco earthquake of 1906. This was caused by movement of a couple of metres along the San Andreas Fault. As in all earthquakes, structural damage to buildings caused by the shaking was made worse by the fires that started as hot coals were scattered and gas mains burst, and the fact that the water mains were broken and hydrants useless.

The most severe earthquake of recent years was the great Alaskan earthquake of 1964. Fault movements took place in an uninhabited mountainous area where the only damage was landslipping. Nevertheless damage in Anchorage, 200 km (150 miles) away, was extensive. Many large buildings were completely demolished, and others were severely cracked and could not be repaired. Timber-framed

buildings fared much better on the whole. Great cracks opened in roads, and railway lines were bent by the movements. Tsunamis lifted boats up on to the quayside in Kodiak, 400 km (250 miles) away, and even killed people in California. This quake was caused by movement on a deep fault in the zone where the Pacific plate pushes down beneath the North American.

The intensity of an earthquake at a particular point on the ground can be gauged according to the damage it causes on a 12-point scale, from 1, where the quake can only be detected by instruments, to 12, catastrophic, where objects are thrown in the air and there is total destruction of buildings. The intensity of an earthquake decreases away from the point where the fault movement takes place. Each earthquake however has a particular magnitude which is related, not to the effects at any one place, but to the total energy released. The Alaskan earthquake had a magnitude of 8·6, San Francisco was 8·25, and Lisbon is estimated at between 8·75 and 9·00.

Much of our knowledge of the inside of the Earth has come from a study of earthquake waves. The speeds that they travel through the different layers, and the absence of shake waves in some places have helped to build up a picture of rocks so deep they will never be seen.

Although it is possible to pinpoint areas which are liable to suffer earthquakes, it is as yet impossible to predict when they will occur.

Left Aerial view of California showing the track of the San Andreas Fault. This is one of the great system of faults at the junction of the Pacific and North American plates.

Right The ruins of Montevago Cathedral, Sicily, after the earthquake of January 1968. Sicily is very prone to earthquakes, lying close to the junction of the African and Eurasian plates.

Volcanoes

There are about five hundred active volcanoes on Earth, of which twenty to thirty erupt in any one year. Some, like Stromboli, are constantly active; others lie dormant for hundreds of years before suddenly exploding. Liquid, solids and gas all come out of a volcano during an eruption, although solid rock is the only permanent record of ancient eruptions. Molten rock, called lava, contains gases such as steam dissolved in it. As lava cools the gas comes out of solution and roars out of the vent to disappear into the atmosphere. The gas is the explosive force behind the eruption and may blow the mountain to pieces. Most volcanoes are very old —Vesuvius has been active for millions of years, for instance—but occasionally a new one is seen to form. On 20 February 1943 a farmer ploughing a field near the village of Paricutin, Mexico, watched a fissure open and grey smoke ascend. As little as ten years after this amazing sight a volcano 200 m (600 ft) high stood on the spot.

Lavas of different compositions vary in their fluidity at different

Above A huge cloud of volcanic ash towering above Vesuvius during the eruption of 1944. It was an eruption like this that buried the cities of Pompeii and Herculaneum in AD 79.

Right A map showing active volcanoes and their relations to plate margins. Hawaii and the Canary Islands are conspicuous in being situated within the stable plate areas.

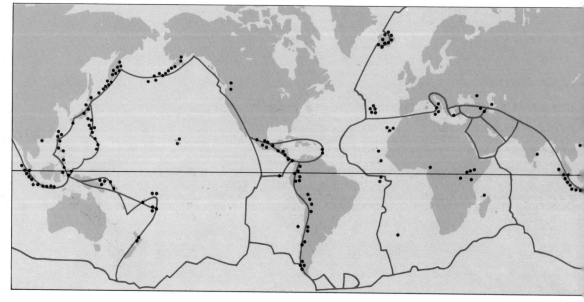

and droplets from the crater, and 'Vesuvian' eruptions where there is some very stiff lava but enormous clouds of ash and dust are also thrown upwards into the air to a great height before falling again.

The largest volcano on Earth is Mauna Loa, Hawaii, which is 110 km (70 miles) across at its base and 10,000 m (30,000 ft) high. This is dwarfed by Mons Olympus on Mars, which is 600 km (350 miles) across and has a summit crater which is 80 km (50 miles) in diameter.

As with earthquakes, most volcanic eruptions take place in the unstable regions of the Earth, such as the mid-ocean ridges, beside the ocean trenches, and in the growing mountain ranges.

Above Strombolian eruption taking place on Mount Etna, Sicily, showing solid, red-hot lava being thrown into the air. This eruption was accompanied by long flows of lava.

Right Basaltic lava on Hawaii, solidified in a form which resembles coils of rope. As the lava cools it develops a skin which thickens and wrinkles as the molten material continues to move.

temperatures, and this affects the course of an eruption. Basaltic lava is quite molten at 1,200°C (2,200°F) and often erupts in spectacular fountains. Gas bubbles out of the cooling lava which flows like water away from the vent. Basaltic volcanoes, which are found mainly in the oceans, are very large, low domes.

Granitic lava on the other hand, is quite the reverse. Although molten at great depth, it is almost solid at the surface even at high temperature. Gas coming out of solution blows the rock to pieces in tremendous explosions, and glowing clouds of red hot ash and gas flow down the steep sides of the volcano, burning all in their path. The Mont Pelée eruption of 1902, when the city of St Pierre was destroyed, was of this type. Between these two extremes are the 'Strombolian' eruptions, where the lava flows slowly and explosions throw clots

Geysers and Hot Springs

When volcanic activity ceases in an active area, rock in the magma chamber below may remain hot for thousands of years. Water circulating below the ground and coming into contact with this rock will rise to the surface as a hot spring. Three volcanic areas have always been famous for their hot springs. These are Iceland, Yellowstone Park, USA, and North Island, New Zealand.

The water that comes out of a hot spring sometimes contains 'juvenile' water, that is, water that has condensed directly from the cooling molten rock underground, and is rich in minerals. For this reason many hot springs have terraces and other deposits of calcium carbonate, silica and sulphur around them. Many springs are reputed to have healing properties, suggested no doubt by their unpleasant taste and smell. 'Taking the waters' was a great feature in the life of gentlefolk in the eighteenth century. While some springs are merely warm, others are extremely hot. Borings at Yellowstone Park encountered steam with a temperature of a scorching 205°C (400°F) at no great depth.

Geysers are hot springs from which fountains of hot water and steam shoot into the air at intervals.

Above Steam and water gushing from a geyser in Yellowstone Park, USA. Notice the wall of mineral surrounding the spout.

Top row, left Terraces of calcium carbonate which formed around a geyser in south-western Turkey.

Top row, right. A diagram showing the rise in temperature in the tubes and caverns below a geyser.

Right An electricity generating station in New Zealand, powered by steam from the rocks underground.

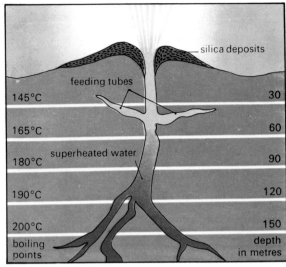

silica deposits

feeding tubes

145°C		30
165°C		60
180°C	superheated water	90
190°C		120
200°C		150
boiling points		depth in metres

The highest geyser spout ever recorded is the 450 m (1,500 ft) achieved by the now extinct Waimangu Geyser in New Zealand in 1901. 'Old Faithful' geyser in Yellowstone Park spurts a 42 m (140 ft) fountain every hour without fail. 'Geysir' in Iceland, after which all the rest are named, regularly spurts to 50 m (160 ft) and is a famous tourist attraction.

A typical geyser is surrounded by a wide pool of water close to boiling point, which has a rim of white silica and calcium carbonate. In the centre of the basin is a pipe, also lined with minerals, which goes down 30 m (100 ft) or more. At the bottom of the pipe the temperature is well above 100°C (212°F). Connected to the pipe are a number of large reservoirs filled with water and steam. The eruption is due to the behaviour of dissolved gases in the water as the temperature rises and pressure is released inside the underground pipe.

The energy available in areas of hot springs has been put to good use in heating houses and even in firing power stations. Many areas that have no natural hot springs have been found to have plentiful supplies of hot water at no great depth. This 'geothermal' energy, used in many parts of the world, such as Iceland, may be an answer to the problems created by the increase in cost of oil as a fuel.

Part 3
WHAT THE EARTH IS MADE OF

Rocks

There are three kinds of rock in the Earth's crust: igneous, sedimentary and metamorphic.

Igneous rocks solidified from a red hot molten 'magma'. They are made up of a mass of crystals of different minerals. Rocks that cooled quickly on the surface of the Earth or under water have microscopic crystals and are glassy; they are found in old lava flows. The slower the rock cooled, the larger are the crystals that make it up. Some granites took millions of years to cool deep underground and have crystals 1 cm ($\frac{1}{2}$ in) across. Igneous rocks poured out on to the Earth's surface through fissures or volcanoes are called extrusive, while those that solidified underground are said to be intrusive. Igneous rocks show a whole spectrum of chemical composition from basalt, rich in iron and magnesium but poor in silica, to granite, rich in silica and aluminium. Basalt and its allies are dark-coloured rocks typical of the ocean floor, though found on land, particularly as an extru-

sive rock; granite and other similar rocks are pale in colour, and very abundant in large intrusions on the continents. The glassy equivalent of granite is called rhyolite; it forms from the glowing cloud in a Peléan type of eruption (see page 51).

Sedimentary rocks form by the weathering, transport and deposition of other rocks. They occupy about three-quarters of the land's surface, but are not found at great depths and make up only a small percentage of the granitic crust as a whole. Sedimentary rocks are subdivided into those that are composed of fragments or grains of other rocks, 'clastic' rocks, including conglomerate, sandstone and siltstone, and those that are precipitated from matter dissolved in water, 'chemical' rocks, including limestone and rock salt. Organic sedimentary rocks are those

Previous page Crater Lake, Oregon, USA, is a basin formed by the collapse of a large volcanic cone.

Left Shale, a soft flaky sedimentary rock formed by the compression of mud on the sea-floor. Shale often contains crushed fossils.

Opposite left Shelly limestone, a chemical sedimentary rock formed by the precipitation of calcium carbonate from sea-water and its incorporation in animal skeletons.

Opposite right Granite, an igneous rock from the depths of the Earth, forming an outcrop in Zimbabwe Rhodesia.

tory. From an igneous rock a geologist can deduce the composition and temperature of the original molten rock and whether it was extruded or intruded. From a sedimentary rock the character of the 'parent' rock that was eroded, the agent of transportation and the environment of deposition can be discovered. In addition, if there are fossils preserved in the rock, one may learn its geological age. From a metamorphic rock a geologist can find out the character of the rock before it was altered, the temperature and pressures responsible for the change and its date.

like coal and shell limestone, formed of fossil animal or plant remains. Shale and mudstone are the most abundant of these, with sandstone second and limestone third.

Metamorphic rocks are formed by the alteration of existing rock by heat and pressure. They make up most of the hidden deep layers of the continents, coming to the surface in the roots of ancient mountain chains. There are two main types. Contact metamorphic rocks are produced by intrusions of molten rock. A fringe of these rocks, the most common being hornfels, surrounds granite intrusions and volcanic pipes. The width of the fringe depends on the length of time the body remained hot. Regional metamorphic rocks are formed over large areas in the roots of growing mountain ranges. In towards the centre of a chain temperature and pressure increase and so different rocks are formed. Rocks, such as gneiss, which form under extreme conditions, are said to be high-grade; those under low temperatures and pressures are low-grade. Sedimentary, igneous and metamorphic rocks can, of course, all be metamorphosed.

A study of the composition of a rock, the minerals present, the overall appearance, the shapes of the grains or fragments and their relations one to another all reveal information about the rock's his-

Right Granite, with large felspar crystals.

Far right Sandstone, a clastic sedimentary rock, made up of grains of quartz cemented by calcite.

Below Basalt, an extrusive igneous rock, outcropping in the Giant's Causeway, Ireland. Regular cracks formed as the cooling rock contracted.

Rocks in Industry

Rocks are used, and have been for thousands of years, in the construction of houses, offices, tombs, bridges, roads, dams, coastal defences and all manner of things which are a part of our civilization. Hard rocks may be cut from the ground in blocks and used as freestone, or they may be broken up, crushed, re-cemented and set in moulds. Soft rocks are baked or otherwise treated before use.

Many different rocks make admirable freestones. Granite is a very hard rock, well suited to large plain buildings, and available in a range of colours from deep pink to white. It is almost unaffected by the weather. Limestone, particularly that of Mesozoic age, may make a lovely freestone which weathers to a pleasant honey-yellow colour. Portland stone from southern England is a famous white limestone, used for such buildings as St Paul's Cathedral, London. Limestones are eaten away by the rain in a polluted, sulphureous city, but can withstand the weather in many other places. Some rocks have specialized uses: marble, for example, is a decorative stone which can be used for indoor panels, while slate is used for roofing.

In areas without any freestones, clay may be dug and baked to make bricks. Indeed, the oldest known buildings, from Ur in Mesopotamia, were built of bricks baked in the sunshine more than 5,000 years ago. Very pure clays are baked to make pottery, some forms of which —'terra cotta' for instance—have been used for building with some considerable success in countries which have hot climates.

The use of freestone, and even to some extent of brick, is now nearly a thing of the past. Most new building, and all major industrial construction, is carried out in concrete. To make this material limestone, sand and clay are powdered together and heated to make cement, and gravel or rock chippings added. Where great strength is required steel rods and netting are built in as reinforcements. This large-scale use of concrete leads to a tremendous demand for raw materials, particularly sand and gravel. Luckily they are easy to extract using large mechanical shovels, and are found in very large quantities in many lowland areas. In Britain more sand and gravel is extracted each year than any other single rock type, and the amount, 110 million tonnes in 1978, has

doubled in the last twenty years, as towns expanded and building programmes became more ambitious. The requirements of the building industry for sand, gravel and other materials will probably continue to escalate in the future.

The building and repair of roads requires rock not only in concrete but in the stone chippings that are used for the foundations and, coated with asphalt, for the road surface. Limestone, igneous rock and sandstone are the three types most often used, limestone being the most important. These same three rocks are used as ballast for railway embankments. Limestone is used in steel-making, in the chemical industry and for agriculture; pure sands and sandstones can be used for glass-making and in iron foundries.

In 1978 300 million tonnes of different types of rock were dug, quarried and mined in Britain. Particularly in small, densely populated countries, the needs of industry and the economy must always be weighed against irreparable damage to the countryside and the very subtle balance of nature. Quarrying and digging are bound to cause pollution of the environment and changes in the ecology of the area which are not necessarily put right when the quarry is 'landscaped' at the end of its working life.

Opposite above Sand-washing plant in a gravel pit, Northern Ireland.

Opposite below Granite being quarried near Baveno, Italy. The large blocks will be used for building and the rubble as aggregate or roadstone.

Left The Houses of Parliament, London, were built in the 1840s, largely of dolomitic limestone from the north of England. The stone was chosen as one capable of withstanding industrial pollution, but not enough trouble was taken to select the best quality stone from within the quarry, and some very inadequate material was used. By 1860 the structure was in poor condition and much stone has since been replaced using a Mesozoic limestone from Clipsham in southern England. This photograph shows the clock tower which holds the famous bell, Big Ben.

Minerals

When examined with care, rocks can be seen to be made up of separate grains of different natural chemicals. These natural chemicals are called minerals. Sometimes the mineral grains in a rock are large and obvious, as in granite. In other rocks, such as basalt or shale, the grains are very small and can only be seen under a microscope: they are present nonetheless. Most mineral grains are either whole crystals or worn or broken parts of crystals. Just a few minerals, such as opal and agate, have no crystal structure and these minerals are said to be amorphous.

Although 2,000 different minerals are known, most common rocks are made up of only seven families of minerals. These, the rock-forming minerals, are quartz, the felspars, the micas, the pyroxenes, olivine, the clay minerals and calcite. Again, although ninety elements are known to occur on Earth, eight of them make up nearly 99 per cent of the rocks of the

Earth's crust. These are oxygen, silicon, aluminium, iron, calcium, sodium, potassium and magnesium. Of these, silicon and oxygen are by far the most abundant, so it is not surprising that quartz, silicon dioxide (SiO_2), is the most common mineral in the Earth's crust.

When it is pure, quartz is a clear, glass-like mineral. When in cavities in mineral veins, it grows as a six-sided crystal with a pyramidal cap. When it forms from molten magma in a rock like granite, it has to fit in amongst all the other grains, so no six-sided columns are to be seen. The irregular grains it does make still have a crystalline structure inside in the way the molecules are arranged in patterns, even though there is no visible crystalline shape outside. Quartz is found in granite

Above A fine specimen of quartz from a crystal-lined cavity.

Left Pyromorphite, a lead mineral that crystallizes in the hexagonal system.

Top right Fine crystals of colourless calcite.

Bottom right Galena, a lead mineral that crystallizes in the cubic system.

and the other pale-coloured igneous rocks common on the continents. It is completely resistant to chemical weathering, so sediment derived from granite will be rich in quartz grains. It is also resistant to change during metamorphism, and therefore quartz grains are very commonly found in metamorphic rocks.

The remaining minerals of the eight, with the exception of calcite, all have oxygen and silicon in their composition and are known as silicate minerals. Felspars, micas, pyroxenes and olivine occur in igneous rocks of different sorts, but as they are vulnerable to chemical weathering, they are found only occasionally in sediments. Mica and felspar are found in sediments that have been eroded from an igneous rock in a dry climate. Olivine weathers very quickly and is almost never found. Of these four mineral groups, mica is easy to recognize because its crystals are glistening black or brown plates like the leaves of a book. It can be seen in any granite, in schist and gneiss, and in the type of sandstone called flagstone. Felspar varies in the amount of calcium or sodium it contains in different igneous rocks, gabbro containing the calcium felspars and granite the sodium ones. They are normally shades of grey or pink and form blocky or tabular crystals. Pyroxenes are dark-coloured minerals that form columnar crystals and are common in dark-coloured igneous rocks like gabbro and basalts; augite is the most common. Olivine is a green mineral found only in dark igneous rocks like gabbro and in volcanic lavas. It is thought to be abundant in the Earth's mantle.

Clay minerals are the aluminium

silicates that crystallize as flakes from the weathering of felspar. The crystals are always tiny and many different clay minerals are mixed in any clay. They are an essential constituent of sedimentary rock. Clay minerals readily alter to other minerals when heated up,

and for this reason they are not found in metamorphic rocks which have been formed at very high temperatures.

Calcite is a colourless mineral which, like quartz, forms six-sided columns with a pyramidal cap. Calcite is softer than quartz and will fizz when a drop of hydrochloric acid falls on it, so they are easy to distinguish. Crystals are found in open cracks and cavities in rock, but calcite is normally found as very tiny crystalline grains or needles in shells, limestone, marble or sandstone.

Although at first sight mineral crystals seem endlessly variable, they can be reduced to six basic sorts, or systems, just as all the different crystals of a particular mineral can be reduced to one ideal form. The systems are cubic, tetragonal (a cube elongated in one direction), hexagonal (a six-sided column), orthorhombic (like a matchbox), monoclinic and triclinic (like matchboxes having sides which are not at right angles to each other).

Minerals in Industry

There are very few minerals for which we have not found some use in the long march of civilization. Copper minerals were mined and smelted about 4000 BC in Egypt, and within the next thousand years copper and tin were being mixed to make the alloy bronze. Iron minerals were smelted in Asia Minor about 1300 BC, and throughout western Europe from 500 BC. The richest and most accessible deposits of these minerals were used first of course, and since then miners have had to dig deeper and deeper, into the Earth making use of poorer and poorer deposits.

Minerals contribute to a vast number of our common household objects. Saucepans, waterpipes, tin cans and electric cables are all obvious enough, but batteries, paints, glass, plaster, pottery glaze, enamel and photographs also all rely on minerals for some stage of their production.

Minerals, as we have seen, either originate deep underground during the cooling and solidifying of a molten rock or the metamorphism of an existing rock, or else at the surface as part of the processes of erosion and deposition. They are normally only of use to us when they have been concentrated by some natural process into a bed, mass or vein which is very rich in a mineral that is rare in the surrounding rock. These natural processes are very slow, so once the concentrated material is removed no more will be produced for a very long time. A mineral that is used for the production of a metal is known as an ore, or as a metallic mineral. Minerals that, although having metal in their composition, are not smelted to produce metal are known as non-metallic minerals. Minerals that occur in large quantities near the ground's surface are quarried in opencast pits, sometimes of enormous size. Those occuring in thin veins or beds are dug from deep mines.

Iron is one of the key elements in our civilization and has been in use for two and a half thousand years. Metallic iron rusts in moist air and is only rarely found as a natural mineral. The oxides—magnetite, hematite and goethite—and the carbonates—siderite and chalybite —are the most important ores. Most iron deposits are sedimentary in origin, being formed in very shallow seawater, though veins are also found associated with igneous rock, as at Kiruna in Sweden. Iron ore is smelted with coke in blast furnaces to produce pig-iron. Carbon is added to make steel, other metals such as nickel and chrome being added in small amounts to give steels of particular properties. The resulting metals can be used in construction, the motor industry, shipbuilding, railways, armaments, machinery, and containers.

Aluminium is the second most widely used metal. It is light and strong and is in demand for the motor industry, construction, electrical components, saucepans and other kitchen articles. Aluminium oxide is an abrasive and a valuable fireproof material in blast furnaces and elsewhere. Aluminium is not found as a natural mineral, and it is bauxite (hydrated aluminium oxide) that is the most important ore. It forms from the chemical weathering of igneous rocks under tropical conditions. It may form a residual deposit replacing the original rock or it may be transported

and laid down elsewhere. Important deposits are found in France, Guyana, Jamaica, Ghana and Australia. Corundum (aluminium oxide) is, apart from diamond, the hardest mineral known, and is crushed for use as an abrasive. Coloured varieties of corundum are valuable as gems (see page 64).

Copper, lead and zinc are the three next most important metals in terms of the amounts used each year, with tin, chromium, titanium, nickel and manganese following.

Of a large number of non-metallic minerals used in industry, sulphur is probably the most important. It is used in the manufacture of sulphuric acid, gunpowder, insecticides, fertilizers, bleaches and in vulcanizing rubber. Natural sulphur is found in beds associated with salt and gypsum which have formed by the evaporation of seawater, and around the craters of volcanoes and geysers. Sulphur is also extracted from metallic sulphides, particularly iron pyrites, and from the hydrogen sulphide gas which is found in oil and gas fields. Because of its wide use in the chemical industry, its consumption is generally regarded as an index of a nation's industrial development.

Fluorite, gypsum and common salt are the next most important non-metallic minerals, with asbestos, felspar, phosphate and potash coming some way behind.

Left The salt works of Salin-de-Giraud, on the south coast of France. Seawater is collected in shallow lagoons and left for the salt to precipitate as the water evaporates.

Above The opencast copper mine at Bingham Canyon, Utah, USA. This deposit contains vast quantities of the copper ore mineral, chalcopyrite, but it is in a very low concentration so enormous amounts of rock have to be processed.

Right Mining machinery at work deep underground. The two arms drill holes in the rock face into which explosive is packed. After blasting, the broken rock is taken away in trucks for chemical processing.

Minerals for Decoration

The seven rock-forming minerals discussed on page 60 are important because, together, they make up the bulk of the Earth's crust. There are also many hundreds of other minerals which, even though they form only a small part of the crust, are of great importance to the human race. Some occur in tiny amounts in common rocks, some are abundant in rare or unusual rock types, others are only found concentrated into mineral veins or masses called pegmatites.

A number of these minerals attracted people's attention from early times for the beauty of their colour or the regularity of their crystal shape. Rarity, beauty and to some extent fashion have governed the esteem in which different minerals have been held and, therefore, the price which they commanded. The most sought-after minerals have always been gems—those that are transparent, can be cut into suitable shapes for wearing, and are hard enough to resist scratches. Many minerals can be cut as gems, but the four most

Right A diagram showing the methods of cutting a gemstone to get the best colour and fire.

Below left A close-up view of a diamond, brilliant-cut, showing the rainbow colours or 'fire'. Diamond has a brightness in its lustre which sets it apart from all other stones.

Below right Crystals of diamond as they are picked from rock debris in the mine.

Opposite above Gold has been mined and treasured for thousands of years. This is the mask of the pharaoh Tutankhamen made in the fourteenth century BC.

Opposite below Two forms of the mineral corundum: **1**) a crystal of ruby unsuitable for cutting; **2**) a cabochon of ruby showing the beautiful 'star' effect given by minute needles in the crystal structure.

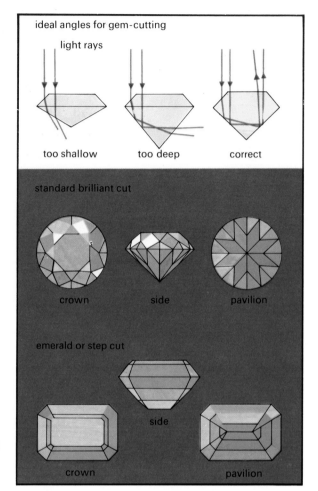

ideal angles for gem-cutting

light rays

too shallow   too deep   correct

standard brilliant cut

crown   side   pavilion

emerald or step cut

side

crown   pavilion

expensive and consistently popular are diamond, ruby, sapphire and emerald. These are the stones which must make up 90 per cent of a high street jeweller's stock, and together represent what most people think of as gemstones. They are set in rings and considered an investment by many people.

Ruby, sapphire and emerald are transparent gems of a rich red, blue and green respectively. Diamond is colourless, or sometimes pale yellow or blue, but has the power to divide up white light into the colours of the rainbow that make it up. A cut stone will sparkle with all shades of red, blue, green and yellow. This phenomenon is shown by other stones as well as diamond and gives 'fire' to the stones.

Among many less-familiar gemstones are peridot, the gem variety of olivine which is yellowish to dark green, tourmaline, whose stones can be green at one end and red at the other, and andalusite, cut stones of which may appear green from one direction and brown from another. Black opal, a variety which shows a play of colours from deep blue through green to red, is another gemstone, even though this mineral is not cut but is polished into a dome, or cabochon.

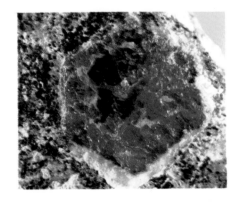

Of the many minerals with an attractive colour that are tough enough to be carved, the best known is jade. This one name covers two separate minerals, jadeite and nephrite. Both occur in a deep green, though jadeite is also found in white, reddish-brown or lilac. It is amusing that a carved figure in green jadeite might be worth several hundred pounds, while the same statue carved in bowenite serpentine, a mineral of very similar properties and colour, only distinguishable from jadeite by careful tests, will not be worth one-tenth of that. Other minerals used for carving are onyx marble (banded calcite formed in stalactites), pale blue turquoise, deep blue lapis lazuli and the organic

mineral amber, made of fossilized tree gum.

As well as these minerals which have a well-established commercial value and fulfill some function in personal adornment or decoration, there are minerals which are collected for their crystal shape or colour, or simply because they are mineral species. These are not generally cut or polished but are preserved in their natural state. In this field there is every gradation of enthusiast, from the rockhound who either goes out to find, or else buys, crystals of quartz or pieces of agate, to the wealthy collector who bids at major auction sales for fine and large specimens of minerals such as malachite, azurite and fluorite.

Fossils and how they Form

A fossil is the remains of an animal or plant preserved in ancient sediment or sedimentary rock. The most ancient fossils known are microscopic plant cells 3,200 million years old, although fossils remain very rare until rocks about 570 million years old are reached, at the base of the Cambrian System. Here easily visible shells are found for the first time. Fossils are forming at the present time in deserts, seas and estuaries, although fossils of interest to the geologist are usually at least several thousand years old. These rather young specimens are not usually turned to stone and often look very like modern seashells, but they are still fossils.

The existence of shells and bones in solid rock has been known for hundreds of years, and all sorts of theories were proposed to explain their presence. Some naturalists refused to believe they were animal remains at all, but thought they were mineral structures or just little jokes of nature. Most people who did accept fossils as the remains of living things thought that they must have been carried far inland and up into the mountains by Noah's flood. Just a few suggested that the mountains were parts of the ocean floor that had been raised up by earthquakes which had occurred in the past.

In addition to these learned opinions there is much ancient folklore associated with fossils which have been used as charms to ward off or cure diseases since earliest times. The well-known fossil oyster *Gryphaea* was known as 'the Devil's toenail', as it looks a little like a misshapen toe. It was used to cure arthritis. Ammonites, known as 'snakestones', were used as a cure for snakebite, and as a charm against the curse of a witch. In China fossil bones were powdered and sold as 'dragon bones', supposedly effective against most diseases.

In any layer of sedimentary rock we may expect to find the fossilized remains of the animals and plants

Left Remains of land animals are very uncommon. This is the skeleton of a primitive reptile from the Permian of Texas, a rare find.

that lived at the time the sediment was being deposited. But fossils give an incomplete picture of ancient life. Only the hard parts of animals are usually fossilized, so soft-bodied creatures like worms or jellyfish will not be preserved, and an animal like a cuttlefish will be represented only by a bone which gives little idea of the whole animal. Furthermore, animals and plants living in, or very close to shallow water are much more likely to be fossilized than those that live on hills and mountains; unless an animal is covered by sediment directly it dies, it is likely to be eaten by scavengers and its bones dispersed over a wide area, leaving no trace.

In spite of this incompleteness, many thousands of different fossil species are known, representing most of the groups of animals and plants that are alive today, as well as many that are extinct and it is with the help of these that we are able to build a reasonably accurate picture of the past.

From the time an animal or plant dies, to the time its fossil remains are collected from the rock, it undergoes changes in parallel with the changing of the sediment, which make the bone or shell look more like the rock that encloses it. Minerals in the rock fill in tiny pores in the fossil, and may completely replace its original structure. In some cases the original structure of the shell dissolves away leaving only an impression, or mould, in the rock to show the size, shape and general appearance of the creature or plant that lay there so long ago.

Top The most common fossils are those of shellfish and other invertebrates that lived on shallow sea bottoms. This sea urchin from the chalk of southern England is a good example.

Above Fossil leaves are preserved in the fine muds laid down in forested swamps. Usually only the impression of the leaf surface is preserved.

Right Often only a few of an animal's bones are found, and the complete skeleton, and then the appearance of the animal in life, have to be reconstructed.

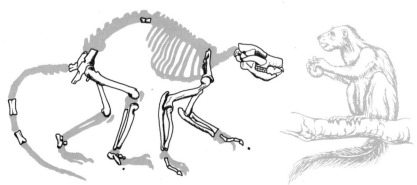

Fossils and Evolution

The first naturalists to study fossils realized that many animals and plants whose remains they found no longer lived on the Earth. What had happened to them, and where were the animals of today in ancient times?

For centuries it was believed that God had created every possible species at the time the world was made and that nothing had been added since that day. It followed therefore that further exploration of the rocks would reveal remains of modern animals, and that in time trilobites and ammonites would be found living in the depths of the ocean. This view died out in the nineteenth century as rock strata and the ocean depths were studied and explored without the expected discoveries.

Other early naturalists believed that life had already been created and destroyed several times in the history of the Earth and that fossils were the remains of a previous creation. They identified the most recent such catastrophe with the great flood recorded in the Bible.

The third theory, which has prevailed, is that of the evolution of plant and animal life from simple cells floating in the surface waters of the sea, to all the living things which inhabit the Earth today. For the early evolutionists, such as Jean Baptiste Lamarck who lived in Paris in the early 1800s, it was seen as a steady progress from the simple to the complex, from the imperfect to the perfect. Our modern ideas about evolution come from Charles Darwin, who published his famous book *The Origin of Species* in 1859. He gathered evidence to show that evolution had taken place, and he suggested a mechanism by which it might have happened.

There are four main lines of evidence which show that plants and animals have evolved. The first comes from the structure of living things. Often a whole group of organisms all possess a particular organ—a flower, limb or mouthparts—which although endlessly adapted for different functions is clearly based on the same plan. In some cases the organ contains parts which are useless to the animal and which can only be explained by evolution from an ancestor that did use them. One example of this in human beings is the appendix. A second line of evidence comes from the internal chemistry of different animals, and a third from the distribution of living organisms around the world, particularly from the peculiar features of those that live on islands and have therefore existed for a long time without

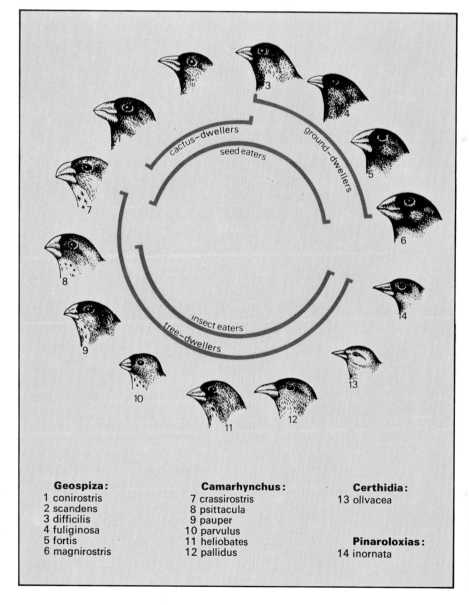

Geospiza:
1 conirostris
2 scandens
3 difficilis
4 fuliginosa
5 fortis
6 magnirostris

Camarhynchus:
7 crassirostris
8 psittacula
9 pauper
10 parvulus
11 heliobates
12 pallidus

Certhidia:
13 olivacea

Pinaroloxias:
14 inornata

Darwin found fourteen species of finch inhabiting the sixteen islands of the Galapagos group when he visited them in 1835. He could only explain their variety by suggesting that they had all evolved from a single pair who made the hazardous 950-km (600-mile) flight from the mainland of South America.

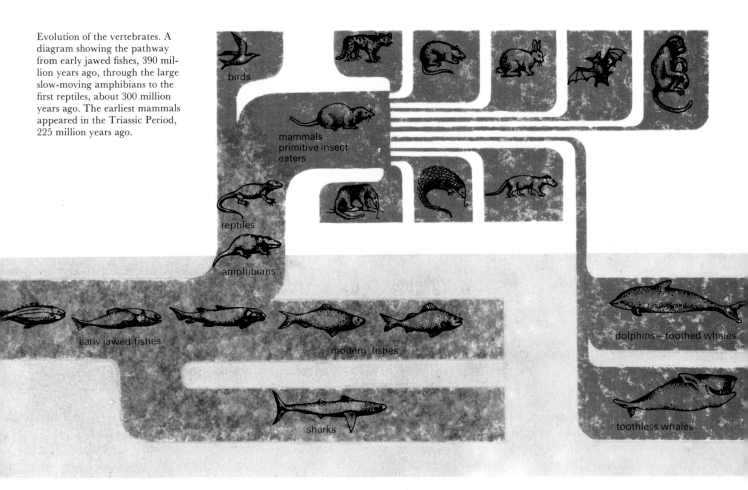

Evolution of the vertebrates. A diagram showing the pathway from early jawed fishes, 390 million years ago, through the large slow-moving amphibians to the first reptiles, about 300 million years ago. The earliest mammals appeared in the Triassic Period, 225 million years ago.

birds

mammals
primitive insect
eaters

reptiles

amphibians

early jawed fishes

modern fishes

sharks

dolphins – toothed whales

toothless whales

new influences being introduced to alter the life-forms which developed over the centuries.

However, the most direct and compelling evidence of evolution comes from the record of past life preserved in rocks. By collecting fossils from successive rock strata we can see the pageant of life unfolding. A pathway has been charted from the bacteria preserved in the 3,200 million year old flinty rock from Swaziland, to the fossil mammals of the Cenozoic Era, a few million years ago. The overall pattern of the origin and extinction of the main plant and animal groups is now well known, and in many cases fossils have been found that are ancestral to two living groups which are now quite distinct. Less commonly, series of fossils have been found in successive beds which show in detail how a particular animal changed over the years. This has been done with sea urchins in the Cretaceous of Britain and with horses in the Cenozoic of North America.

Darwin's theory, which we still accept, is 'natural selection'. Living things produce many more offspring than eventually survive, and these offspring are not identical, but vary. This variation affects their ability to survive in particular environments. The offspring most able to survive will not die young, and will pass on their own particular variation to their own offspring. Over many generations there is a constant selection of variations beneficial to the organism, and a gradual change of structure will take place. This constantly increasing adaption to environment is what we mean by evolution. In this way animals and plants develop special means of protection against enemies or a harsh climate. Speed, camouflage, colouring and climbing ability have been perfected to ensure the survival of the fittest in any species.

Below This is *Archaeopteryx*, the skeleton of the earliest-known bird, from the 130 million year old Solenhofen Limestone of Bavaria. Although this animal had feathers and could probably fly, it had many reptilian features and is a true 'missing link'.

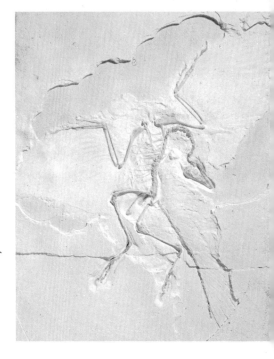

The Importance of Fossils

Fossils are not only a fascinating record of life in the past, they are of real importance to the geologist searching for oil and gas or attempting to reconstruct the history of the Earth. Because of the steady progress of evolution, each geological period had its own type of life, and therefore the rocks laid down in each period contain fossils peculiar to them. The canal engineer William Smith first realized this about the year 1800 when he found that each of the rock units around Bath, England, had a characteristic set of fossils, distinct from those above and below them. He used this discovery to trace the units right across England, and in 1815 published the first large-scale geological map of any country in the world, *A delineation of the strata of England and Wales, with part of Scotland*. This map would have been more difficult to make and more liable to error without the use of fossils.

The use of fossils has been steadily extended and refined since

Above A bed of fossil ammonites, extinct animals related to the living nautilus. Ammonites are used to correlate Mesozoic rocks.

Right Modern grains of pollen. Pollen grains are very tough and can be perfectly fossilized in rocks millions of years old. Being very tiny, fossil pollen grains are easily recognized in samples from boreholes.

Below left A fossilized trilobite that lived during the Cambrian Period, just over 500 million years ago.

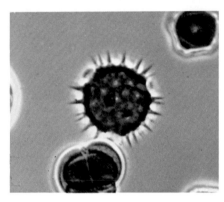

Smith's day. Instead of looking at all the fossils from one bed geologists concentrate on particular types that are known to have evolved very rapidly and to have lived in many different habitats over wide areas. Trilobites are used in the Cambrian System, graptolites in the Ordovician and Silurian, and ammonites in the Jurassic and Cretaceous. The range of these fossils from one bed of rock to the next must be found out by careful collecting, and then a number of different species can be named as 'indexes', each one characterizing a narrow band of rock known as a zone. The Silurian System is divided into twenty-four zones, each one named after its own index graptolite, which are found over much of the northern hemisphere. A zone

is always the same age wherever it is found and whatever type of rock the fossil might be in.

The whole procedure of determining the relative ages of rocks in different parts of the world is known as correlation. It is obviously of fundamental importance to any understanding of the ancient geography and climate of the world. How would we begin to reconstruct the geography at the beginning of the Silurian Period were it not for the fact that the *Glyptograptus persculptus* zone has been traced throughout Europe and into other areas. At least we know what the environment must have been like in these areas.

Of more economic importance is the fact that fossils allow us to distinguish between the many other-

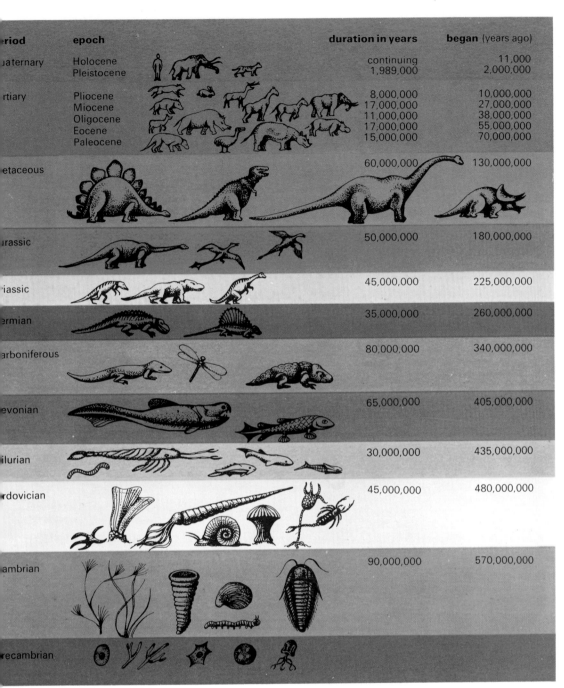

riod	epoch		duration in years	began (years ago)
uaternary	Holocene		continuing	11,000
	Pleistocene		1,989,000	2,000,000
rtiary	Pliocene		8,000,000	10,000,000
	Miocene		17,000,000	27,000,000
	Oligocene		11,000,000	38,000,000
	Eocene		17,000,000	55,000,000
	Paleocene		15,000,000	70,000,000
etaceous			60,000,000	130,000,000
urassic			50,000,000	180,000,000
riassic			45,000,000	225,000,000
ermian			35,000,000	260,000,000
arboniferous			80,000,000	340,000,000
evonian			65,000,000	405,000,000
ilurian			30,000,000	435,000,000
rdovician			45,000,000	480,000,000
ambrian			90,000,000	570,000,000
recambrian				

This diagram of the life of the past shows how each of the geological periods had particular sorts of animals and plants, different from those above and below. The subdivision of the geological column into periods is based on changes in particular fossils. The dates in the columns are based on the radioactivity of minerals (see page 78). Of the animal and plant drawings notice particularly the early trilobite and brachiopod (lamp shell) in the Cambrian, the first fish in the Silurian, the giant dragonfly in the Carboniferous, the first bird in the Jurassic, and *Homo sapiens* right at the top, in the Quaternary.

wise identical rock units in the geological column. When searching for coal by sinking boreholes, it is important to be able to distinguish the beds of rock just above the coal from those just below. The first contain one sort of coiled shell which means there is hope; the second contain a different sort of shell and that means there is none. Where all exploration is done by boreholes, as in the search for oil and gas, it is much more convenient to use very small fossils as a guide to age. They are much more likely to be recognizable in chipped and broken rock than are trilobites or ammonites.

One type of microscopic fossil which is used a great deal is the foraminiferan, a coiled shell a fraction of a centimetre across. In similar ways fossils can be used in the search for building stones—different brachiopods are found just above and just below the famous Bath stone in south-west England for example—and in the location of water supplies—different sea urchins are found at the top and bottom of an important water-bearing rock layer in southern England.

How much money the landowners of the last century would have saved had these simple facts been understood! These days, fortunately, full use is made by miners and land developers of the knowledge built up by geologists concerning the formation and history of the Earth's crust throughout the last 4,600 million years.

Fossil Fuels

Living plants grow by using energy from the Sun to build complex organic molecules in a process known as photosynthesis. Animals get their energy for growth by eating green plants or other animals. When living things die they are either eaten, or decay through the action of bacteria, and the energy in their chemical structure is passed on. In certain conditions, particularly where oxygen is in short supply, organic material will not rot but will be preserved for millions of years. We use this fossil organic material as a source of energy; it is often known as fossil fuel.

The first fossil fuels to be widely used were peat and coal. In swamps and bogs plant material often builds up faster than it can rot in the stagnant water, and thick deposits of dark brown peat may form. This is cut into blocks, dried and used as fuel in areas like Ireland where it is very abundant. Beds of peat which become covered with layers of clay and sand gradually change to coal as the swamp water is squeezed out of them, and they become richer in carbon as gases are driven off. Peat buried to about 3,000 m (9,000 ft) turns into a compact brown material, still with occasional recogniz-able twigs, that contains 70 per cent carbon and is called lignite. The richest coal, anthracite, is 95 per cent carbon and must have been buried at 6,000 m (18,000 ft).

The peak period of coal formation was the Upper Carboniferous, 300 million years ago, when swampy forests of giant reeds and ferns covered much of Europe and North America. Periodically these forests were drowned by the sea, so coal is found typically in seams a metre or two thick, separated by sandstones and shales. Coal seams close to the surface are dug from gigantic open pits; deeper levels are reached by mines.

Energy locked up in the soft parts of animals is also stored up under certain circumstances and can be used as fuel. Such organic materials which become trapped in sediment in stagnant water are attacked by

Above Both coal and oil can be used to generate electricity for lighting, heating and industry. This station is under construction in Wyoming, USA.

Left An oil rig used for drilling in shallow water.

Above right Modern rotary cutters can dig and transport 100 tonnes a day from a thick coal seam. A skilled operator, protected by a hard hat, mask and safety lamp, keeps watch over the controls.

Right A diagram showing the many ways that the main derivatives of coal are used. These are usually forgotten when coal and coal mining are discussed.

when drilled, have proved barren, while others have yielded millions of barrels of oil. As oil flows out of the reservoir to the surface, water flows, or is pumped, in to take its place, so there is no danger of underground collapse.

The crude oil which comes from an oil well is a mixture of hydrocarbons which can be separated in a refinery to yield petrol, paraffin oil, lubricating oil, paraffin wax, bitumen and many other materials, each of which has its particular uses. The lightest hydrocarbons of all, the natural gases such as methane and ethane, can be piped straight to the consumer for use as fuel and are used for cooking and heating.

Coal and oil are both being formed today in stagnant waters in swamps and on the seabed, but they are forming very much more slowly than we are using them up. Unless alternative sources such as solar energy are found to be practicable, there will be an energy crisis throughout the whole world before we are far into the next century.

bacteria that can live without oxygen and are turned into the mixture of hydrocarbons that we call oil. As the sediment becomes more deeply buried it is compressed, and the oil droplets and seawater tend to be pushed out into porous rocks like sandstone. Oil is less dense than water, so the droplets tend to run together at the top of the porous bed. If the bed has been bent up to form a dome, then a very large amount of oil, and perhaps gas as well, may be trapped under pressure. The sediment where the oil originated is known as the source rock. The first oil fields to be discovered were found by digging wells in areas where oil seeped to the surface from an underground reservoir. Over the last few decades, with the demand for oil rising all the time, geologists working for oil companies have searched, both on land and under the sea, for suitable dome structures in porous rocks. Many of these structures,

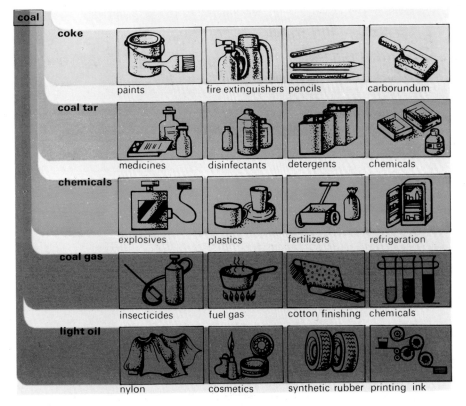

coal

coke — paints, fire extinguishers, pencils, carborundum

coal tar — medicines, disinfectants, detergents, chemicals

chemicals — explosives, plastics, fertilizers, refrigeration

coal gas — insecticides, fuel gas, cotton finishing, chemicals

light oil — nylon, cosmetics, synthetic rubber, printing ink

Part 4
THE
STORY OF
THE EARTH

Reading the Layers of Rock

The rocks we see in cliffs and quarries, or discover by drilling, give us most of our knowledge of the history of the Earth. A geologist is trained to tell a story from even the most ordinary-looking piece of rock.

Sediment, whether in a lake or on the bed of a shelf sea, is generally laid down in flat layers, one upon another, the oldest always being at the bottom. As we have seen, these layers may be broken and bent by underground forces, so the geologist's first job on coming to a new area is often to sort out the original order of deposition of rock layers. Then each of the rock layers must be studied in turn, starting with the oldest, noting the minerals in the

Previous page Castner Mountain, Arizona, USA, is made up of bedded rocks that can tell the geological story of the area.

rock, the shape and size of the grains and the form of the layering. Any fossils in the bed must also be recorded. Using knowledge of the rivers and seas of the present day, the geologist can then assess the environment in which the sediment was laid down, not only the depth of water but also how far it was from land, and maybe even something about the source, weathering and

transport before the sediment was even laid down.

Normally rocks with grains of sand or gravel were laid down in shallower water than those with silt grains or fine mud. A rock whose bedding planes are covered with ripple marks, like those of sand on a beach, was certainly a shallow-water deposit. Very fine shale containing fossils of floating

by the evaporation of seawater and are usually found among red desert sandstones, indicate hot, dry conditions and the drying up of large inland lakes.

From such clues, information is slowly gathered about the climate and geography of the past. By using fossils to relate beds of the same age in different areas a wider ranging picture can be built up. When this information from the sedimentary rocks of the land is linked to what we know of the drift of the continents through Earth's history, as discovered from studies of the seafloor, we will have a good idea of the changes that have occurred on the surface of the Earth. Add to this information gleaned from the folding, faulting and metamorphosis of the sedimentary rocks, and the intrusion of igneous rocks, and our knowledge of the Earth will be complete.

Far left Crystals of anhydrite, a mineral that forms from evaporating seawater.

Left The bedding lines in this quarry face are not straight but curved, showing that the sandstone was once a desert sand dune.

Above A rock surface scratched and polished by the movement of an ancient glacier. The shape of the scratches can show which way the glacier was moving.

Right The Grand Canyon, Arizona, USA, where more than a kilometre of undisturbed strata have been exposed by the rapid erosion of the Colorado River.

and swimming animals only, with no sign of burrowers, was probably laid down in deep water with a stagnant bottom. Although rocks formed in river deltas and on shelf seas make up the bulk of the geological column, other environments are also represented, such as desert sand dunes, glacial moraines, lake clays, pebbly beaches and deep-ocean oozes.

Special features in a rock can give a clue to climate. Unfossiliferous sandstones coloured red by iron oxide with a characteristic curved bedding are thought to have been laid down in ancient deserts. Irregular masses of stones, sand and clay with no obvious bedding, and associated with the scratching and polishing of the rocks below, were laid down by melting glaciers and so indicate a very cold climate. Beds of coal usually suggest a hot climate where vegetation would grow very fast and luxuriantly. Beds of minerals, like common salt, which form

Dating Rocks

Dating rocks has always been a great problem for geologists. Using fossils, a complicated series of periods and ages have been built up, as we shall see later, but fossils can give no clue to the actual age in years of a rock. Ask a geologist how old a particular rock is and he will say something like 'Lower Carboniferous'. This is a name based on the fossils in the rock; until the beginning of this century we had no idea whether the Lower Carboniferous was five or 500 million years ago.

The earliest estimates of the age of the Earth came from a study of the Bible. Three hundred years ago, working back through all the generations recorded in the Books of Chronicles, Archbishop Ussher of Armagh, in Northern Ireland, calculated that the world was created in 4004 BC. This date was printed as a marginal note in the Authorized Version of the Bible, and was accepted for many years. A more scientific method was proposed by Edmund Halley in 1715. He tried to work out the length of time it would have taken for the sea to get to its present saltiness, assuming that it had started out quite fresh and that the flow of the world's rivers had remained more or less constant. Unfortunately he did not publish his results. Yet another attempt was made in Paris by Count Buffon in the 1770s. He made a large sphere of iron to represent the Earth, heated it until it glowed white, which he thought was the state of the primeval Earth, and left it to cool to the temperature of the Earth today. His sphere took a period to cool which, after elaborate calculation, suggested to him that the Earth was seventy-four thousand years old. These and other geological methods were tried with no great success until the beginning of this century, when the real key was found.

Radioactivity, the emission of particles and radio waves by the atoms of certain elements, was discovered in 1896. It was found that individual atoms in any radioactive sample 'decay' at a fixed rate, giving off a tiny amount of radiation and turning into a stable, non-radioactive element. Some elements are highly radioactive and

Below A uranium mine in Canada. Pitchblende is the most important ore uranium and Canada is one of the world's major producers.

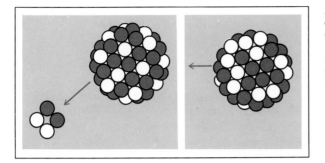

Left A diagram showing the decay of an unstable atom of the radioactive element uranium. A tiny particle is given off and a stable atom of the element thorium is left.

Above The delicate analysis needed for radioactive dating is carried out by this instrument, a mass spectrometer. It can measure tiny quantities of the different varieties of a particular element very accurately. This one is used at the Institute of Geological Sciences in London, England.

decay very rapidly: a pure sample of a particular type of the element radon will have almost completely decayed to polonium at the end of one second. The elements useful in geology are those which take thousands of millions of years to decay. If a pure sample of one of the types of uranium had been prepared when the Earth was formed, then today nearly two-thirds of it would have decayed and, by measuring the rate of decay of the piece that was left, we could easily calculate the age of the Earth. In practice of

course, it is a little more difficult.

The radioactive elements which are found in rocks and which are used in dating are uranium, found in uranium ores, rubidium, found in a wide range of igneous and metamorphic rocks, and potassium, found in volcanic rocks. In addition, and used in a rather different way, there is carbon-14, used for dating archaeological materials. No rocks on the Earth's surface date back to the origin of the Earth, the oldest that has been found so far is a metamorphic rock from Greenland that is 3,750 million years old. The world was already old by then.

Apart from giving at least a minimum figure for the age of the Earth, radioactivity allows us to date the geological periods worked out by

fossils. There are very few sedimentary rocks that can be dated in this way; they usually give the date of the formation of the pebbles and grains that make them up, and not the date of the laying down of the sediment. Where beds of lava or volcanic ash are laid down in among layers of sediment, then the date of the lava must be very close to that of the sediments. Sometimes it can be shown that an igneous rock intruded a sediment soon after it was formed, so here again some sort of a date can be given. The rarity of such cases, together with the analytical error which is present in all age calculations based on radioactivity, means that fossils will continue to be the main means of correlating the rocks in which they occur. The geologist will continue to think of Lower Carboniferous as the age of his rock sample, even though he knows it is round about 340 million years old.

The fossiliferous rocks are divided into eleven systems, the oldest being the Cambrian. Below the Cambrian are thick masses of sedimentary and metamorphic rocks which were lumped together as the Precambrian. Radioactive dating has revealed that these rocks were formed over a period of more than 3,000 million years, five times as long as the time represented by the fossiliferous rocks! By dating metamorphic rocks on the great Precambrian shield areas of Africa, Asia and Canada, it is now possible to recognize a number of major time divisions within this long period, so that correlation of rocks from one continent to another is possible.

Radioactive carbon is present in the air in tiny amounts and is taken up by plants and by animals. Once it is fixed as part of a leaf or bone then it is not replenished from the air and starts to decay to become stable nitrogen. Because it decays relatively quickly this method of dating cannot be used on materials more than about 50,000 years old. Wood, peat, shell, bone, hide and fabric can all be dated in this way.

The Geological Column

Just as human history can only really be grasped when subdivided into easily remembered periods based on reigns or parliaments, so the history of the Earth must be subdivided. Geologists have based their subdivisions on the fossils found in the various rock layers, so the first division is into Phanerozoic —rocks containing visible life— and Precambrian. The Phanerozoic is divided into three parts, Cenozoic, Mesozoic and Palaeozoic— rocks containing recent, middle and ancient life. Each of these is subdivided into a number of systems which are the most important of all the divisions. Unfortunately many of the eleven have long and difficult names which beginners in geology find quite off-putting. But all the names have a meaning which can aid the memory. Carboniferous is the age of coal, and Cretaceous of chalk. Permian is based on rocks near Perm in Russia, and Devonian on rocks in Devon, England.

Each of the eleven terms can refer either to a period of time or to a mass of rock laid down in that time. So the Ordovician Period is a span of time just like the Victorian Age, and the Ordovician System is all the rock laid down during that time—

just as buildings and furniture are called 'Victorian'. Finer subdivisions of the eleven are called series, then stages, and finally zones (see page 79). Series and stages are usually named after the areas where their rocks were first described, and zones after the index fossil.

Today all these terms are very carefully defined, and special committees have to be consulted before old names can change their meaning or new ones be introduced. A hundred years ago things were much less organized, and there were frequent disagreements about the meaning of these terms. The two most famous British geologists of the nineteenth century were Roderick Murchison and Adam Sedgwick. Murchison studied rocks in South Wales and named the Silurian System at the same time as Sedgwick studied rocks in North Wales and named the Cambrian. It was quite soon discovered that the upper part of Sedgwick's Cambrian was in fact the same age as the lower part of Murchison's Silurian. The two men argued all their lives, both sticking stubbornly to their respective systems. It was only after they had both died that another geologist, Charles Lapworth, suggested making a new

system, the Ordovician, out of the overlapping beds.

Even today there are still some disputes. The boundary between the Cambrian and the Ordovician is taken at one level by some geologists and at another by others. In America the rocks between the Devonian and the Permian are divided into two systems, the Pennsylvanian and the Mississippian, while in England there is the single Carboniferous System. The very top of the geological column is also rather a muddle, with Tertiary and Quaternary being used instead of Cenozoic and so on.

Systems can be recognized all over the world, but that is not true of the smaller subdivisions. Some fossil zones can be traced across several continents, but because fossils, like living animals tend to inhabit one particular area of the globe, few if any are really worldwide, and some are only found in a single country. Stages are more widespread than zones, but again, seldom worldwide. For this reason each country and continent has developed its own scheme of these finer subdivisions. It is the eventual aim of the geologist to replace all these with a single scheme which will represent a detailed correlation of fossiliferous rocks all around the world.

The best that can be said about the jumble of irregular names and only half-understood concepts that make up the geological column is that in practice it works, providing the geologist with just the frame of reference needed to do the job.

The Great Sphinx at Giza in the United Arab Republic, with the pyramids of Myceries (*left*) and Cephren (*right*) in the background. We consider the Sphinx (built *c* 2900–2550 BC) an ancient structure, but compared with the geological age of the Earth, it is very young indeed. It is, however, a fine example of the enduring quality of stone as a building material.

	Era	Period	Date millions of years	Plants and Animals	Geological Events
Cenozoic					
	CENOZOIC	Quaternary		Extinction of large mammals after the Ice Age; *Homo sapiens* appears.	Ice ages affected North America, northern Europe and Asia. Low sealevels elsewhere.
70			2		
Mesozoic	CENOZOIC	Tertiary		Mammals evolve to dominate the land.	The Alps, Andes and Rocky Mountains formed; Greenland split from Europe.
225			70		
Palaeozoic	MESOZOIC	Cretaceous		Dinosaurs become extinct at the end of the period; flowering plants evolve.	Inland seas and swamps in North America, a great delta and then open sea in Britain. Chalk laid down over much of Europe and North America.
570			130		
	MESOZOIC	Jurassic		Dinosaurs dominate the land, though small mammals and birds are also found.	Shallow seas over Britain and the western USA; the Atlantic Ocean gradually opens.
			180		
	MESOZOIC	Triassic		The first dinosaurs, ichthyosaurs and mammals evolve in this period.	Hot desert over much of northern Europe, most of North America also above water.
			230		
	PALAEOZOIC	Permian		Many ancient groups, including trilobites and rugose corals, become extinct.	Appalachian and central European mountains formed. Continents united in a single mass, 'Pangaea'.
			270		
	PALAEOZOIC	Carboniferous — Pennsylvanian / Mississippian		Great forests of giant tree ferns and horsetails develop at the end of the period. Reptiles evolve from amphibians.	Much of North America and Europe low and swampy.
			350		
	PALAEOZOIC	Devonian		Plants and later insects colonise the land for the first time. Amphibians evolve from fish.	Clear warm seas very widespread, with many coral reefs.
			400		
	PALAEOZOIC	Silurian		Coral reefs develop in Britain, giant water scorpions and small fish live in freshwater.	Mountains up-raised in northern Britain, Scandinavia and the eastern USA.
			440		
	PALAEOZOIC	Ordovician		Fish evolve, but invertebrates, including trilobites and brachiopods, dominate the sea. There is no life on land.	Shallow seas covered huge areas. Volcanic activity in Britain, glaciation in the Sahara Desert.
			500		
	PALAEOZOIC	Cambrian		Many groups of shellfish, trilobites and sponges evolve.	North America joined to Scotland as one continent, England joined to the rest of Europe.
Precambrian			600		
		Precambrian		Microscopic algae existed 3,500 million years ago, soft-bodied animals evolved at the end of the period.	
Origin of the Earth 4,600					

The Age of the Earth

The oldest rocks so far discovered on the surface of the Earth are from Isua, West Greenland, where a metamorphic rock, the Amîtsoq Gneiss, has been dated by its radioactivity to 3,750 million years. The same region has a conglomerate containing pebbles of volcanic rock which seem to be even older. So not only was there solid crust on the Earth at this time, there was even running water able to roll pebbles along. Rocks of this date have been found at a number of other places including Minnesota

Right Amîtsoq Gneiss, the oldest rock in the world, dated at 3,750 million years.

Below An artist's impression of the face of the Earth 4,500 million years ago when the molten surface was beginning to crust over.

in the USA, Swaziland, central Australia and the Antarctic.

Other evidence of the age of the Earth comes from outer space. Stony meteorites have been dated by their radioactivity to around 4,600 million years. It is thought that they originated within the Solar System between the orbits of Mars and Jupiter, and there seems every reason to believe that the entire Solar System formed as a whole at one time. This idea is confirmed by the discovery of a few pieces of coarsely crystalline rock on the Moon, which once again yield dates of about 4,600 million years. This rock seems to be part of the original crust of the Moon and is quite different from the lavas and breccias that make up most of the surface. The Earth is so much more active than the Moon that all its primeval crust has long since been destroyed by plate movements.

The age of the Earth is so vast that it is almost impossible to comprehend. If 4,600 million years is scaled down to one single year, the world being formed on the 1st of January, then the beginning of the Cambrian Period, 570 million years ago, would be 16 November. Dinosaurs would not appear until about 15 December, while the first human would not be on the scene until a few hours before midnight on the last day of the year.

The early history of the Earth is still largely unknown, but we do at least know its outlines. Condensation of part of the vast cloud of cold dust and gas that gave rise to the Solar System formed the Earth, a large part of it molten from the energy of impact of gigantic rocky fragments, and the Moon orbiting around it. As it cooled the Earth was surrounded by a very thick and dense atmosphere of gases such as carbon dioxide and carbon monoxide, but at a very early stage this was all stripped away by the force of gigantic outbursts from the growing Sun. This left both Earth and Moon unprotected from meteorites, many of them enormous,

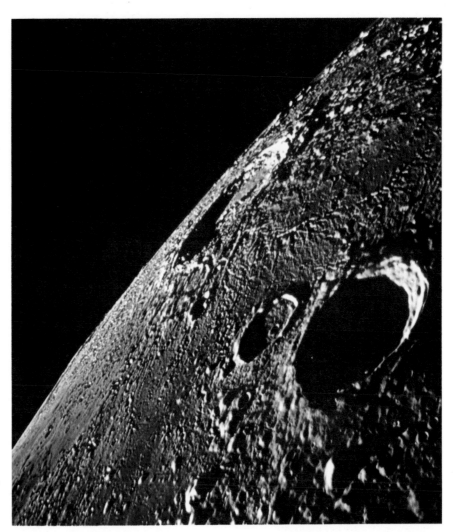

The Moon, photographed by the Apollo 12 astronauts. Unlike Earth, the Moon has been geologically inactive for 3,000 million years, so many of its surface features and rocks are very ancient. Pieces of the original 4,600 million year old crust have even been found.

which crashed in from space. The gigantic craters on the Moon date from this time; those on Earth have long since disappeared. As the globe cooled two things happened. Minerals began to crystallize from the melt and sink down towards the centre. Iron and nickel crystallized first and sank fastest to form a central core of metal, and basic igneous rocks like gabbro began to make a crust over the surface. As the crust thickened, small patches of granite appeared on the surface as the basic rocks were repeatedly broken and remelted. These patches of granite were to be the first continents.

As the molten rock solidified gases, including water vapour, carbon dioxide and nitrogen, were given off and began to build a new atmosphere around the Earth. The water vapour condensed to form thick clouds and fell as rain, starting the processes of erosion and sedimentation and the build up of lakes, seas and oceans. This was the stage at which the Amîtsoq Gneiss formed, 3,750 million years ago.

The small granitic continents continued to grow, and moved over the Earth, propelled by convection currents in the soft mantle. Occasionally two would collide and join together. Primitive living cells evolved in hot volcanic pools at a very early stage, and 2,000 million years ago plant cells capable of photosynthesis evolved to add oxygen to the atmosphere. Earth's major features had appeared.

The Palaeozoic Era

The oldest fossil animals are found in Australia. They were soft-bodied things like jellyfish, worms and sea slugs, and very different from anything alive today. The rocks they are found in are thought to be about 600 million years old. The first animals with hard shells are found in rocks about 570 million years old, and their appearance marks the beginning of the Palaeozoic. First come tiny brachiopods and snails, then sponges and tube-shaped hyolithids. A little later the first trilobites appear. The earliest animals are all small and thin-shelled, but by the middle of the Cambrian some at least achieved a length of 30 cm (1 ft). There must have been seaweeds alive at the time, but almost nothing is known about them at the present time.

The first traces of vertebrates are found in Ordovician rocks. No skeletons have been found, only tiny but unmistakeable fragments of fish scale. The oldest complete fish come from the Silurian. Only a few centimetres long, they have no proper jaws, only a ring of muscle around the mouth, just like the modern lamprey. The land must have been a barren rocky wilderness at this time, but early in the Devonian the first plants evolved that could live on the land, though only on wet and swampy ground. At the same time insects and scorpions left the water and took to the land. The vertebrates followed a little more slowly, and it was not until the very end of the Devonian that one group of fish evolved walking limbs and lungs to become the first amphibians, able to live both on land and in the water and thus increase their chances of survival.

The geography and climate changed continually throughout the 340 million year long era. At the start there were four continents, Europe, North America, Asia and Gondwanaland, but at the end of the Silurian Europe and North America collided, the force of the impact raising a range of high mountains through Scandinavia, Scotland and the eastern USA. These, now much eroded, are the mountains of Norway, the Grampian Highlands of Scotland and the Appalachians of North America. About 280 million years ago, at the end of the Carboniferous Period, the three remaining fragments all collided and joined to form one enormous mass, the supercontinent of 'Pangaea'. Land was continuous from the North Pole to the South and half-way round the Equator.

In one or two areas we get glimpses of the Palaeozoic climate. Traces of an ice age have been found in Ordovician rocks in what

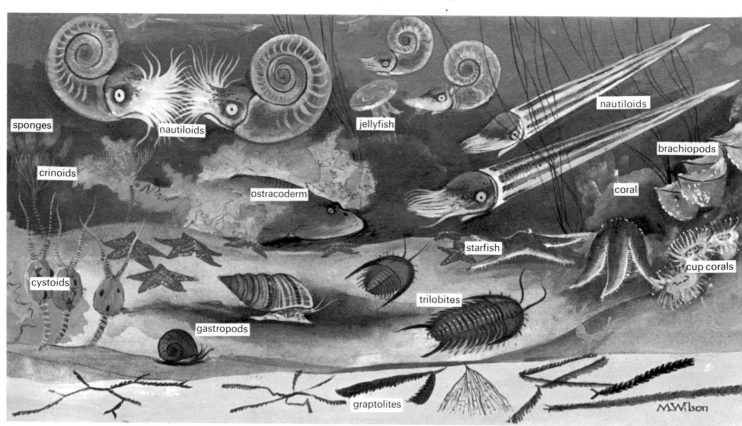

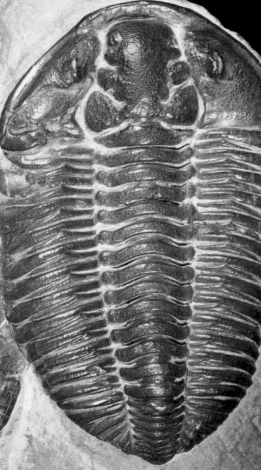

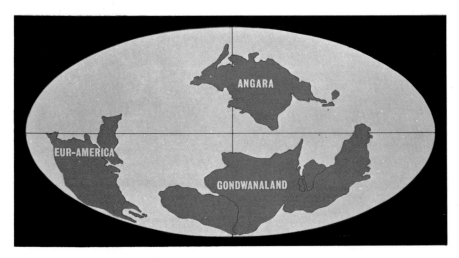

Left Reconstruction of life on the seafloor during the Ordovician Period. Animals are shown in their living position except for the graptolites which would have been floating in the surface waters. A primitive jawless fish, an ostracoderm, lurks among weeds in the background.

Above left Beautifully preserved graptolites from the Ordovician Period of Scotland. Each black graptolite is a colony which once contained a tiny soft animal living on each of the protruding teeth.

Above right This trilobite, given the scientific name *Calymene blumenbachi*, is found in the Silurian limestones of central England. It is so common around the town of Dudley that it is known as the Dudley Locust.

Centre A diagram of the continental drift in Lower Devonian times.

is now one of the hottest parts of the world, the middle of the Sahara Desert. From the scratches on the rock surfaces below the stony and sandy moraine deposits, it is even possible to map out the direction of flow of the ancient glaciers.

The middle Silurian limestones of Britain contain a number of large coral reefs, rich in brachiopods, trilobites and molluscs of all kinds. The presence of so many different species living together suggests warm water; corals in particular are known to flourish only in the warm. The Carboniferous began warm over Europe and North America where dense low-lying forests covered the land, something like the coastal rain forest in the tropics today. At the very end of period an ice-cap developed over an enormous area centred on the ancient South Pole. The discovery of glacial beds of this age on the now separated fragments of Pangaea—India, South Africa, South America, Australia and the Antarctic—was one of the first pieces of evidence for continental drift. The Palaeozoic ended with the formation of an enormous hot desert

stretching from Britain through Europe and into northern Africa and the United States. In all these areas fossil sand dunes and thick deposits of salt have been found to aid geological deduction as to the history of these landscapes.

Through most of the Permian in these areas the only fossils to be found are the footprints of early reptiles, occasional freshwater fish and the leaves and stems of plants. There were only very small areas of shelf sea on the edges of the super-continent, the period being a time of very low sea-level. Perhaps for this reason the end of the Palaeozoic is marked by the extinction of many animal groups which were probably unable to cope with life under these conditions. However, some species did survive, bearing out Darwin's theory of the survival of the fittest and the law of natural selection.

The Mesozoic Era

In most parts of the world the rocks of the Triassic System, which marks the start of the Mesozoic, look much like those of the Permian, but in fact in the few places where shelf-sea deposits can be found, the fossils are very different. Like the Permian, the Triassic was a time of low sea-level with a hot desert covering much of the northern hemisphere. At the end of the Permian many of the old groups of shellfish had become extinct, leaving the seas half empty. The Triassic was a time of steady evolution of the new forms which became much more widespread in the enormous shelf seas in the Jurassic and Cretaceous. On land too the faunas had changed. During the Permian the reptiles had evolved to look very like mammals, particularly in the structure of the lower jaw, but during the Triassic most of these became extinct, leaving one group to evolve into small shrew-like animals that were the first real mammals. Another quite unrelated group of reptiles evolved very rapidly into a multitude of forms—the dinosaurs who were to dominate their age.

The Jurassic Period saw a steady rise in sea-level until shelf seas covered much of the supercontinent. In these seas lived ammonites, belemnites, sea urchins, six-rayed

Above A very characteristic rock, laid down over much of Europe during the late Cretaceous, is chalk. This is a pure white limestone made up of the skeletons of minute plants called coccolithophores.

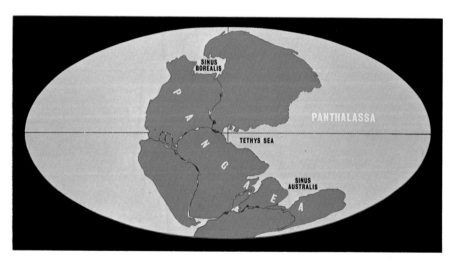

Below The world as it was 170 million years ago in the Jurassic Period, showing the continents in a single enormous mass.

corals, oysters and many other such small creatures who found the new conditions congenial to the survival of their species.

Two groups of reptiles made their way back to the sea and evolved into the long-necked plesiosaur and the dolphin-like ichthyosaur. On land new groups of plants, the cycads and conifers, took over from the ferns which dominated the Palaeozoic, and flowering plants appeared for the first time in the Cretaceous. Mammals remained small and insignificant throughout

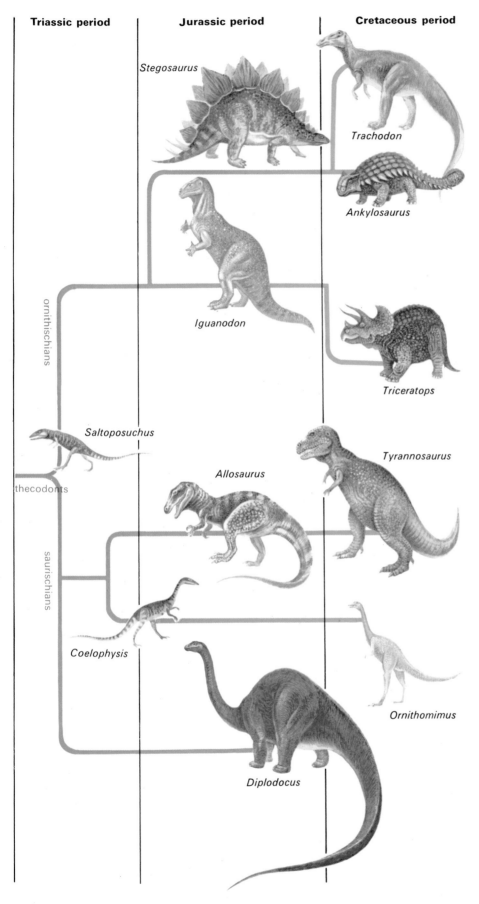

Stegosaurus

Trachodon

Ankylosaurus

ornithischians

Iguanodon

Triceratops

Saltoposuchus

Tyrannosaurus

thecodonts

Allosaurus

saurischians

Coelophysis

Ornithomimus

Diplodocus

the Mesozoic, living on insects, small lizards and eggs. It was the dinosaurs that ruled the land. There were small ones the size of chickens; there were plant-eaters 25 m (75 ft) long that must have weighed upwards of 70 tonnes; there were plant-eaters protected with thick bony armour; there were the meat-eaters like *Tyrannosaurus*. The dinosaurs have captured the imagination of the public, and are probably better known than any other extinct animals, making a tremendous impact on literature and especially the cinema. Two of the most spectacular were *Stegosaurus*, with its cluster of strange armour-like panels along its spine (perhaps a cooling system), and *Diplodocus* whose immense bulk and distinctive long neck and tail have made it a natural model for artists' impressions of the Loch Ness monster. An important event in the history of life was the appearance of the first bird at the end of the Jurassic. Birds are very like dinosaurs in many features of their skeletons, and they may well represent a group of dinosaurs that took first to the trees and then to the air.

The supercontinent of Pangaea remained unchanged until about 130 million years ago when it began to break up and the present pattern of continents and oceans appeared for the first time. The Atlantic Ocean first began to open up between Europe and North America, and Africa and South America broke away from Antarctica. India, having once nestled between Africa and Australia, was an island at the end of the Mesozoic, steadily drifting northwards towards Asia.

The main feature of the Mesozoic climate was its uniformity. There seems to have been little difference from the Poles to the Equator; certainly nothing like the very strong zoning of the present day.

Left The evolution of the dinosaurs was the main event of the Mesozoic as far as life on Earth was concerned. Mammals remained small and inconspicuous while the giant reptiles flourished.

The Cenozoic Era

This is the age of mammals. Dinosaurs became extinct at the end of the Cretaceous, and the mouse-like mammals, overshadowed throughout the Mesozoic, evolved rapidly into many shapes and sizes. Flying, swimming and meat-eating forms all existed early in the Cenozoic. The egg-laying mammals of Australia, the duck-billed platypus and spiny anteater, are living descendants of the primitive Mesozoic forms. Primates, a group having eyes at the front of the head and hands able to grasp, evolved at the beginning of the Cenozoic, and included monkeys and apes by the middle. *Homo sapiens*, our own ancestor, evolved in Africa about fifteen million years ago, and had become a widespread and accomplished toolmaker by about two million years ago.

The Cenozoic saw the continuing drift of the fragments of Pangaea; the Atlantic Ocean widened steadily and Australia broke away from Antarctica about fifty million years ago and moved northwards. India, an island, moved north until, about eight million years ago, it collided with Asia, raising the Himalayas. At the same time the northward movement of Africa towards Europe narrowed the Mediterranean and raised the Alps. The great ranges of the Rockies and the Andes rose during the later part of the Cenozoic as the Pacific seafloor plate pushed against the western edges of North and South America.

The end of the Cenozoic Period was marked by great and rapid changes of temperature, particularly in the northern hemisphere. During the last two and a half million years the pattern of the ocean currents has often changed and cold water from the Arctic has poured south, cooling the lands it passed and affecting the animals and plants of the northern seas. At least four times the cooling was so severe that ice-caps built up over Canada, northern Europe and northern Siberia. The glaciation of 400,000 years ago was the hardest, with an ice-cap well over 1,000 m (3,000 ft) thick reaching as far south as Brittany in France. The present climate, with the two polar ice-caps and strong temperature zones from Poles to Equator, shows that there

Below A selection of land animals of the Cenozoic Era.

Right A mountain in the Grampian Highlands of Scotland showing signs of glaciation in its rounded outcrops and deep, ice-scoured lake.

may be more cold weather on the way in the not too distant future —according to the geological timescale, that is. By the timescale of the history of civilization and the human race, the next ice age is a long way off yet in the future of the Earth. At present it is something which only concerns scientists.

Glossary

Abrasion The wearing away of rock by repeated small impacts. Sand grains carried by the wind abrade rock outcrops in deserts.

Ammonite An extinct marine animal, related to the living squid and nautilus, that possessed a coiled shell.

Asteroids Rocky and metallic bodies circling the Sun between the orbits of Mars and Jupiter, possibly the broken remains of a planet.

Basalt A fine-grained igneous rock that is rich in iron and magnesium and is dark in colour. It makes up much of the ocean floor and is a common lava on land.

Block Mountain A small range made of flat-lying rock layers, separated from the surrounding plains by a major fault.

Boulder Clay An unsorted sediment of clay, sand and angular rock fragments laid down from melting ice; also known as 'till'.

Brachiopod A small marine animal that has a shell in two unequal parts. Rather uncommon today, though very abundant in the Palaeozoic and Mesozic Eras.

Calcite A crystalline mineral, calcium carbonate, occurring as limestone, in the shells of animals, and as crystals in fissures and cavities in rock.

Carbon-14 A radioactive form of carbon which is produced in the upper atmosphere. It is the basis of radiocarbon dating of archaeological samples.

Chondrule Tiny blob of silicate mineral found in certain stony meteorites.

Cirque A steep-walled bowl close to a mountain peak which was once the starting point of a glacier.

Clastic Rock One made of fragments or grains of other rocks and minerals, e.g. conglomerate and sandstone.

Climate The average weather conditions of an area, measured over a period of years.

Continents In common terms the six great landmasses of the world are the continents. Geologically speaking they are the rafts of granitic crust (sial) that rest on the basaltic crust. Most of the continental surface is land at present.

Continental Drift The slow movement of the continents at speeds of about 1 cm ($\frac{1}{2}$ in) each year that is caused by convection currents in the mantle.

Convection Rise and fall of a fluid caused by a temperature difference between the top and bottom of a vessel.

Core A ball of nickel-iron alloy 3,400 km (2,100 miles) in radius at the centre of the Earth. It is at a temperature of 10,000°C (18,000°F) at the centre.

Correlation Working out the relative ages of sedimentary strata in different parts of the world. Strata are said to correlate if they can be shown by their fossils to be the same age.

Crust The outermost of the Earth's rocky layers which has a continuous basaltic layer (sima) which supports the raft-like granitic continents (sial).

Crystal A natural geometric shape assumed by a freely growing mineral which is a reflection of the internal arrangement of atoms. There are six basic crystal systems.

Delta A thick mass of sediment which has formed around the mouth of a river.

Desert An area which has less than 25 cm (10 in) of rain each year and in which few plants or animals are to be found.

Dune A ridge or crescentic body of sand that is moved along by the wind.

Earthquake The shaking of the land that occurs when rocks move along an underground fault. The movement sets off push-pull, shake and long waves which travel out, getting weaker all the time.

Evolution The steady change in plant and animal life through geological time as organisms become adapted to an ever-greater range of habitats and environments.

Fault A crack in the rocks of the crust caused as strata on either side are being displaced.

Felspar A family of rock-forming silicate minerals that form blocky or tabular crystals. They are common in igneous and metamorphic rocks.

Fold A bend in a rock layer caused by lateral pressure, usually when the rock was deep underground.

Fold Mountain Long and narrow mountain ranges made of folded sedimentary, igneous and metamorphic rocks, which form as moving oceanic crust pushes against and crumples the edge of the continent.

Fossil Remains or trace of an animal or plant preserved in ancient sediment or sedimentary rock.

Freestone Rocks that can be cut into blocks and used for building.

Galaxy A cluster of a thousand million or more stars spread over a hundred million light years, and separated from other clusters by empty space.

Geothermal Energy The heat energy which is available underground, particularly in areas of hot springs.

Geyser A hot spring that regularly shoots a fountain of water and steam into the air.

Glacier A tongue-shaped river of ice which flows down a valley from a mountainous area of high snowfall.

Gneiss A metamorphic rock rich in mica, formed by the high-grade metamorphosis of mud.

Granite A coarse-grained igneous rock that is rich in silica and aluminium and is pale colour. It is a common intrusive rock in the continental crust.

Graptolite Small fossils shaped like saw blades that were once colonies of tiny marine animals. Graptolites have been extinct for 380 million years.

Gravity The attractive force that acts between any two bodies. The Earth has a field of gravity around it which gives us all weight.

Hornfels A rock formed when mud or shale is metamorphosed at high temperature but under no great pressure. It is found surrounding igneous intrusions.

Iceberg A mass of ice floating in the

sea, nine-tenths of which is hidden below the surface.

Igneous Rock Rock which solidified from red hot magma, either on the surface (extrusive) or underground (intrusive).

Index Fossil A fossil which is used as a guide to the geological age of a rock layer and which gives its name to a particular zone.

Island Arc A line of volcanic islands, usually making a gentle curve, which develops on the landward side of an ocean trench.

Joint A crack in the rock along which no displacement has occurred.

Karst Topography The landscape developed in limestone areas where rivers run in underground caves and solution features develop.

Lava Fine-grained extrusive igneous rock, either erupted from a volcano or from a fissure in the ground.

Lignite Low-grade coal, containing about 70 per cent carbon, formed when peat is buried to a depth of 3,000 m (9,000 ft).

Loess A fine-grained dust deposit which forms around the edge of large deserts.

Longshore Drift The movement of sand and pebbles along the shore due to waves approaching the shoreline obliquely.

Magma Molten rock generated underground, particularly at plate margins.

Magnetic Field Movements in the outer core of the Earth result in it being a gigantic magnet with poles close to the geographic poles. The Earth's magnetic field protects us from cosmic radiation.

Mantle A layer, probably of peridotite rock, 2,900 km (1,840 miles) thick lying around the Earth's core and below the crust.

Meander A wide bend in a senile river. Meanders change in shape as rivers undercut their banks on the outside of bends.

Metamorphic Rock Rock formed by the alteration of igneous or sedimentary rock by heat and pressure. Slate, marble, schist and gneiss are well-known examples.

Metasomatism The chemical changes that occur as debris changes into rock. Chemical change during metamorphism is also called metasomatism.

Meteor The streak of light in the sky

caused by a small meteorite passing through the upper atmosphere.

Meteorite A fragment of rock or metal thought to be derived from the asteroid belt which, captured by our field of gravity, lands on Earth.

Moraine A mound of boulder clay formed at the sides or snout of a glacier.

Natural Selection A theory explaining how evolution occurs first proposed by Charles Darwin. In each generation variants best suited to a particular environment will survive there, and the form of the organism will progressively change.

Ocean Basins In common terms the five great open seas of the world. Geologically speaking they are the low-lying areas between the raft-like continents.

Oil A mixture of hydrocarbons derived originally from the soft parts of animals and plants. Crude oil is refined to yield petrol, paraffin, wax and bitumen.

Pangaea The single continent that was in existence from the Permian Period, 250 million years ago, until the late Jurassic, 140 million years ago.

Peat Plant remains preserved in stagnant water. Thick peat deposits are forming in many poorly drained areas, particularly central Ireland.

Planets The nine rocky and gaseous bodies that, along with their satellites, orbit the Sun and make up the Solar System.

Plate A slab of crust and upper mantle about 100 km (60 miles) thick which is rigid and stable. Fifteen plates make up the Earth's surface at the present time.

Plate Tectonics The theory which includes continental drift and sea-floor spreading and explains the distribution of fold mountains, volcanoes and earthquakes in terms of plate collision and formation.

Quartz A crystalline mineral, silicon dioxide, occurring in granitic rocks, as crystals in fissures and cavities in rock, and as clastic grains in sandstone.

Radioactivity The emission of particles and waves by the atoms of certain elements. Rocks and minerals can be dated from their natural radioactivity.

Ridge A mid-ocean ridge is an

underwater mountain range, the site of earthquakes and volcanic eruptions, and marks the line of a rising convection current in the mantle.

Sea-floor Spreading The formation of new oceanic crust along the mid-ocean ridges means that sea-floor is constantly being pushed away from the ridge on either side.

Sedimentary Rock Rock formed by the weathering, transport and deposition of the debris of other rocks and minerals.

Shelf Sea A sea not more than 180 m (500 ft) deep which covers the edge of a continent.

Soil A layer of rock and mineral fragments and humus in which microscopic organisms live and plants grow.

Solar System This consists of the Sun, nine orbiting planets with satellites, the asteroids, and the comets.

Speleologist A student and explorer of caves.

Stalactite An icicle-like growth of calcium carbonate hanging from the roof of a limestone cave.

Stratification The layering which is noticeable in most sedimentary rocks. One layer is often called a stratum, and the science of rock layers and their age is called stratigraphy.

Swallow Hole A funnel-shaped depression in a limestone area where a stream disappears underground.

Tide Rise and fall in sea-level that occurs twice each day and is caused by the fields of gravity of the Moon and the Sun.

Trench An ocean trench is an elongated depression on the ocean floor, the bottom of which is at a depth of 11,000 m (7 miles), and which marks the line where a plate is sinking down into the mantle.

Trilobite An extinct marine animal distantly related to the living king crab. Trilobites have been extinct for 250 million years.

Volcano A mountain made up of layers of ash, dust and lava which periodically erupts, emitting gas, lava and rock fragments.

Wave An oscillation of the water surface produced by the wind blowing over open water. When a wave approaches the shore it becomes more pronounced and breaks against the land.

Widmanstätten Structure The feathery pattern of intergrown crystals visible on a polished and etched surface of an iron meteorite.

Zone A thickness of sedimentary rock characterized by the presence of a particular index fossil which indicates its geological age (see page 80).

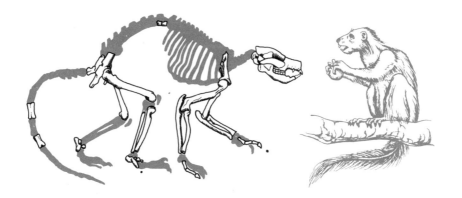

Index

ridge, mid-ocean 20, **91**
river 36
roadstone 59
rock 56, 58
   cycle *47*
   forming minerals 60
   fall 36
rounded particles 43, *43*
ruby *65*

Sahara Desert 28, *40, 42*
salt *62*
   dome 47
San Andreas Fault 46, *48*
San Francisco Earthquake 47, *48*
sand and gravel 58
sand dune 28, *42*, 43, *76*
sandstone 56, *57*
sapphire 65
Saturn 13
schist 45
sea, shelf 19, 22
   urchin *67*
   floor spreading 20, **91**
seasons 17
Sedgwick, A. 80
sedimentary rock 56, **91**
senile river *36*, 37
series 80
shale 44, *57*
shelf sea 19, 22, **91**
shelly limestone *56*
shield 25
shooting star 14, *15*
sial 19
siderite 62
Signs of the Zodiac 10
Silurian 81, 84
sima 19
sink hole 39
slate 45

Smith, W. 70
snakestone 66
soil 35, *35*, **91**
Solar System 8, *8*, **91**
solstice 17
sorted sediment 42, 43
space rocket *13*
spectrometer *79*
spectroscope 10
speleologist *39*, 38, **91**
Sphinx, Great *80*
spit 42
stage 80
stalactite *38*, 39, **91**
stalagmite 39
star 10
star stone *65*
steel 62
strata 44
stratification 44, 76, **91**
Stromboli, Italy 50
Strombolian eruption *51*
sulphur 63
Sun 10
Surtsey, Iceland *6*
swallow hole 39, **91**
systems, crystal 61
   geological 79, 81

temperature, highest 28
terra cotta 58
Tertiary 81, 88
thunder 31
tide 22, **91**
time measurement 17
tourmaline 65
trade wind 30
transport of sediment 36, 40
trench, ocean 22, **92**
Triassic 81, 86
trilobite *70, 84, 85*, **92**

Tropic of Cancer 17
tsunami 48
turbidite 23
turquoise 65
Tutankhamen's mask *65*

U-shaped valley *27*, 41
unconformity 47, *47*
uplift 46
Ural Mountains, USSR 26
uranium 79, *79*
uranium mine *78*
Uranus 13
Ussher, Archbishop 78

Van Allen Belt 17
variable star 10
Venus 13
Vesuvius *50*
Vesuvian eruption 51
volcanic island 23
volcano *6*, 50, **92**
   world map *50*

Waimangu Geyser, New Zealand 53
water, work of 36
   cycle *30*
wave 22, 32, **92**
   erosion 37
weather 30
weathering 34
westerlies 30
Widmanstätten structure 14, **92**
wind 30
   work of 40

Yellowstone Park, USA *52*
youthful river 37

zone 70, **92**

Acknowledgments

The author and publisher would like to thank those who have given their permission for illustrations to be reproduced in this book. All diagrams are reproduced by permission of Orbis Publishing Limited unless otherwise credited. The diagrams on pages 18, 21, 22, 24, and 45 were prepared by Bridgewater and Grain.

Aldus Book 38*t*

J. Allen Cash 42*b*

Ardea 51*b*, 53*tl*, 56*r*, 69*b*

Barbagello/IGDA 51*t*

Barnaby's Picture Library 41, 54, 89

Bevilacqua/IGDA 57*t*, 58*b*, 70*b*, 70*t*

British Museum 67*t*

British Tourist Authority 59

Camera Press 17, 50*t*, 64*bl*, 72*b*, 78, 83

Cirani/IGDA 36*l*, 63*t*

De Beers/IGDA 64*br*

Doulton & Company Limited 34*b*

Ganna/IGDA 77*t*

GEGB 79*t*

Hale Observatory 8*t*, 9*t*

IGDA 13*t*, 40*b*, 60*t*, 60*b*, 61*t*, 61*b*, 63*b*, 65*t*, 70 *centre*, 76*l*

Icelandic Photo and Press Service/IGDA 6

Institute of Geological Sciences 14*b*, 38*b*, 44*t*, 47*t*, 56*bl*, 57 *centre*, 57*b*, 58*t*, 76*r*, 79*b*, 82*t*, 82*b*, 85*tl*, 85*tr*, 85 *centre*, 86*b*

A.F. Kersting 80

Leonardi, Pinna/IGDA 66

McCutchen /IGDA 43*t*

Marka/IGDA 24*b*, 52*l*, 77*b*

Meunch/IGDA 34*tr*

Mitchell Beazley 12, 13*b*

Mount Wilson Observatories 10

National Coal Board 73*t*

Diana Nyllie, J. Allen Cash 39*t*

ONST/IGDA 40*t*

Orbis *half-title* 8*b*, 9*b*, 11, 15*b*, 16*l*, 18*b*, 19, 20, 23, 29*t*, 30, 31, 35, 36*r*, 37*b*, 39*b*, 43*b*, 44, 46*b*, 47*b*, 50*b*, 53*tr*, 64*tr*, 67*b*, 68, 69*t*, 71, 73*b*, 84, 87

Ostman/IGDA *title page*, 37 *centre*, 72*t*

Ostman, Cirani/IGDA 37*t*

Picturepoint 12, 16*r*, 28, 29, 34*tl*, 49, 52*r*, 74

Poggio/IGDA 42*t*

Science Museum 15*t*

SEF/IGDA 86*t*

Seaphot 22*r*

Spectrum 14*t*, 25, 45*b*

Spence Air Photos/IGDA 48

Tony Stone/IGDA 62

Swiss National Tourist Board 27

Titus/IGDA 46*t*

Tomish/IGDA 65 *centre*

Ward Lock 18*t*, 21, 22*l*, 24*t*, 45*t*

ZEFA 32

USDA 88